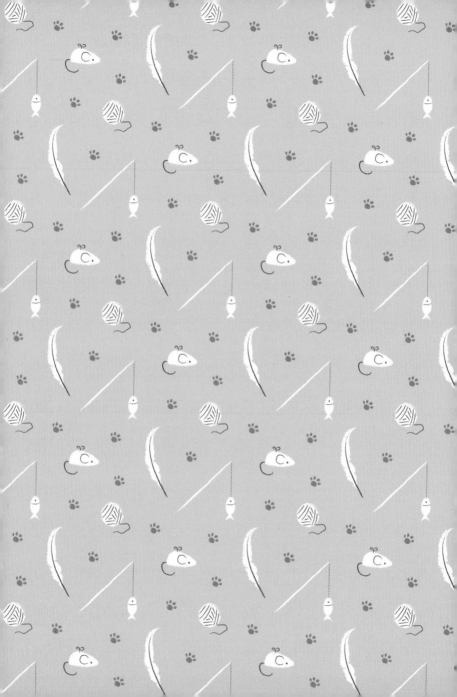

THE CAT LOVER'S A TO Z

Clare Faulkner

THE CAT LOVER'S
A TO Z

Hardie Grant

QUADRILLE

INTRODUCTION

I have always been a cat person – they make me indescribably happy – and if you are reading this little book, I am sure you are an ailurophile too (head straight to the 'A' section if in doubt). I hope you will enjoy weaving through this A to Z of all things feline and sharing in the joy these furry creatures bring us. While it is intended as a light-hearted rather than a serious guide, I do hope it provides some helpful advice along the way. You could dip in and out or read it from A to Z, it is entirely up to you, but ideally do it with a cat curled up on your lap.

Double trouble

I was lucky to grow up with a pair of half-Abyssinian troublemakers – the oddly named Flip and Scamp – and it would not be an exaggeration to say they were my best fur-iends as a child. Although they were rivals at home, together they terrorized the neighbourhood and, to our shame, were even accused of stealing a whole roast chicken from a neighbour's dining table. Once Scamp infamously escaped from a cattery but was thankfully returned to the family some days later in a sorry state. Flip wisely declined the opportunity to join him on that occasion. They were a steady, fluffy presence through my teenage years, and they gently mellowed in their old age. They left a cat-shaped hole in my heart.

After many years of trying to accost random cats in the street, along came Cookie, an old-style Siamese cat with way too much cat-titude. It would be fair to say we all worship at his fuzzy feet and he has assumed his rightful position as the boss of the household. I fear we constantly disappoint him with our inability to provide entertainment deemed exciting enough. By the evening he has generally given up and chooses a lap to snooze on, which must first be assiduously evaluated for its suitability. Cookie has given us our share of sleepless nights, once spending the night in freezing temperatures stuck ten metres up a tree, eventually to be rescued by a gallant tree surgeon. He is surely an adventurer at heart! He also happens to be so incredibly beautiful that I could stare at him all day; but he'd hate that, so I must ration my adoring glances. He has been very helpful in the creation of this book and is proud to be credited as one of the 'cats involved in the making of this book'.

See AILUROPHILE, ABYSSINIAN, ALL-NIGHTERS, MISDEEDS, NEIGHBOURS, TREES

ABYSSINIAN

These gorgeous almond-eyed cats with handsome ticked coats and cute tufted ears look like miniature wild-cats and are renowned for their supreme intelligence and playfulness. Some Abys are even reported to play fetch, as long as there is a fitting reward on offer!

ACCESSORIES

You might get your kitty to tolerate a pirate costume or a lion's mane for a few nanoseconds, but take it from us, you're wasting your hard-earned pennies. Attempting to get that all-important snap for social media is not for the faint-hearted. Cats are professionals at holding grudges, and humiliating outfits could put you in your moggy's bad books for the rest of the day. In our experience, a bow tie firmly attached to their collar at Christmas is about as exciting as it gets.

Accessorize at your own risk

ACROBATICS

Most cats will not jump through hoops for anyone or anything. Nevertheless, even the laziest of cats has an impressive array of anti-gravity moves that will occasionally surface – from the classic forward roll to the mid-air jumping spin – to impress even the most jaded cat-owner. These feline feats of agility are strictly spontaneous and under NO circumstances will they be repeated for a camera or an adoring audience.

ADOPTION

With so many cats needing homes, consider using a reputable shelter to find your purr-fect match. Adopting an adult cat and offering them a loving new home will bring you both heaps of joy. An older cat is likely to be more chilled once settled and a lot less trouble than a spirited kitten, but shelters also have kittens looking for homes, if that's what your heart desires. Sometimes a cat will choose you as its new owner by turning up on your doorstep and making its feelings known. If you've done everything possible to make sure you're not taking someone else's beloved moggy – including asking a vet to check for a microchip, postering the local neighbourhood and attaching a paper collar to the cat with your details on – and come up with nothing after seven days, it is likely to be the start of a beautiful new friendship. #adoptdontshop *See also* RESCUE

AGEING

Just like humans, cats will slide into old age with varying degrees of dignity and their waistline is likely to be the first place to reveal their advancing years. With less time for hunting and much more for snoozing, you may need to consider dusting off the kitten toys or bringing a new diet to the table. On the plus side, your senior kitty is likely to be more laid-back than they were in their youth and will appreciate your warm, inviting lap more than ever. *See also* CHONK

A laid-back oldie

*Most cats will jump
through hoops for no one*

AGILITY

Believe it or not, cat agility is the
feline sporting equivalent of show
jumping for horses and there are
competitions where trained cats
show off their skills at mastering
obstacle courses. It's hard to imagine how
it could work without them, but a-paw-rently
treats are strictly forbidden. *See also*
ACROBATICS, TRICKS

AGOUTI

In this case not the large rat-like creature, though
we're sure your cat would be more interested in these, but the gene
that produces hair shafts with bands of light and dark colour and gives
the tabby cat their distinctive striped hairs.

AILUROPHILE

A fancy word for you: a person who loves cats. *See also* CAT LADY

ALLERGY

Some cat lovers are so dedicated to their moggies they are willing
to endure a long list of eye-watering symptoms, from sneezing and
wheezing to coughing and rashes. As it is generally the dander flying
around the home that is the cause, it is possible to reduce symptoms
with military-style tactics, including cat brushing and bathing (good
luck with that one), air purifiers and meticulous cleaning. There
are also cat foods available that can reduce the allergens your cat
produces, and other scientific solutions are in development, giving new
hope to sneezy cat fans.

ALL-NIGHTERS

Whether they've got themselves locked in a shed, stuck up a tree or are just pushing the boundaries, your outdoor cat will test your nerve at some point by pulling an all-nighter. If it's your first time, you are likely to spend an all-nighter too – fretting. To avoid a sleepless night, check neighbouring gardens, trees and garages before you go to bed. Don't forget your cat could also be messing with your head and hiding inside your home, oblivious while you frantically ransack the neighbourhood. Chances are they will swan in for a quick snack in the morning and saunter out again as if nothing has happened. *See also* LOST, YOUTH

AMERICAN SHORTHAIR

A strong, chunky cat with short ears and an adorable round face, they are renowned for good health and an easy-going nature. Likely to be good mousers as they are thought to be descended from ships' cats.

ANGER

If you are lucky enough to own a cat with a big personality, you are likely to end up with a sourpuss at some point. Whether they are bored or not getting enough attention, are overstimulated or irritable, cat behaviourists tell us it's best to try to ignore a hiss-terical cat. This can be easier said than done when you are backed into a corner or teetering on a staircase, stalked by a little devil. In this situation, distraction or surprise will get you out of most tense moments. Punishment does not help the situation, so reinforce good behaviour with attention and ignore the bad. Anger could also be a sign of fear or being unwell, so don't ignore out-of-character aggression in your cat. *See also* FIGHTING

ANXIETY

While cats can seem very laid-back, they love routine and familiarity, so even little changes to your habits or your home can stress them out. Some cats haven't had proper socialization as kittens, or may have some issues from their past, and this can lead to an anxious pussycat. If your cat gets upset when you are out, don't make a big fuss when you leave the house, consider leaving the radio on and keep them busy with a slow feeder that makes them work hard for their biscuits. Pheromone sprays and diffusers are a great way to spread some calming vibes around the home. Let your cat pick up on your own relaxed cat-titude and they may follow your lead. If you have tried the above to no avail, or if your cat is weeing in inappropriate places or overgrooming, it is worth seeking your vet's advice, as these can be signs of stress that need further intervention.

AQUARIUM

A tank of fish might seem like a great way to keep your demanding cat entertained, but it could be a rather stressful situation for the fish. If you really must have an aquarium, prevent your cat from pawing at the glass, give the fish a place to hide and make sure the cat can't get on the top, which is dangerous for everyone involved. A tank that your angling angel can't reach could be a happy compromise or consider playing fish videos on cat TV.

Spare a thought for the fish

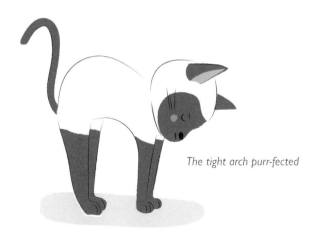

The tight arch purr-fected

ARCHING

Cats are very bendy indeed and will give any yogi a run for their money. The tight arch, often seen after a long snooze or a lengthy sit down, is a classic invigorating stretch for the flexible feline. You may also see your cat arching when about to pounce in play or when it's getting serious and warning you or another cat to back the hell off. *See also* STRETCHING, YOGA

ASIAN

A shorthair group that includes the Burmilla, Asian Self, Asian Smoke, Asian Tabby and the longer-locked Tiffanie. These pretty cats with soft and glossy coats are Burmese in type but not colour and have large, enchanting eyes.

ATHLETIC

When your cat is vegging out after a hard day's doing nothing at all, it can be difficult to believe their big cat relatives are among the speediest creatures on earth. However, it might surprise you to learn the humble house cat at their peak can beat the fastest humans.

ATTACK

It is very cute when your kitten unleashes a playful attack on you but it's not so funny, a few months later, when your now enormous floofball decides you make an excellent toy and ambushes you with a surprise attack, claws and teeth at the ready. A bored cat may be more likely to stalk you, so pre-empt attacks with plenty of active play. Look out for signs that your cat is getting over excited – such as a thrashing tail and ears going flat – and end a play session before it goes too far. *See also* ANGER

ATTENTION

Many people think cats are anti-social but most of them love company, at least for some of the day, and if they're not getting enough, they will find myriad clever ways to engage your attention. If you are leaving the house, you can guarantee your moggy will perform an irresistible belly flop at your feet to delay your exit. If you are attempting a lie-in at the weekend, your cat may stand on your head or miaow in your face. If you are trying to work, they may sit helpfully on your keyboard. No one is more expert at getting attention than our feline friends. *See also* ANGER, MISCHIEF, WFH

BALANCE
Unless you have a decidedly chonky cat, your cat should
have perfect balance and will make light work of any fence or
ornament-strewn shelf. Cats will use their claws, sensitive paws,
tail, inner ears, flexible back and shoulders, and growing experience
to navigate the narrowest of ledges. We can all learn from those light
little feet placed purr-fectly in front of the other. Despite this, even
the most skilful cat can slip up, but if they have enough time to right
themselves, they are likely to land better than a professional gymnast.
See also ACROBATICS, FALLS

BALD
Probably the only cats that will
welcome a fluffy jumper, the most
famous of the bald cats is the Sphynx.
They are not completely hairless but
are covered with a velvety layer of soft
down. These controversial but striking
kitties make up for their lack of fluff with
big purr-sonalities, but they will need
dedicated care for their skin and are
highly sensitive to the sun and the cold.
See also ALLERGY, SPHYNX

BALINESE
Like a longer-haired Siamese, with the
distinctive dark points, large ears and
piercing blue eyes, but with less of the
chat. Lavish them with attention and you
will be fur-ever friends.

BASKET

The old-school wicker baskets for visits to the vet and cattery, while sturdy and generally tamper-proof, are rather unwieldy, hard to store, and likely to trigger a stampede to the cat flap on sight. Some say doubling them up as a cat bed works a treat and avoids the panic problem, but your cat will likely turn their nose up and choose your bed instead. *See also* CARRIERS, VETS

BATHS

Most cats will agree, this entry should not appear in a cat dictionary and, indeed, our furry friends don't generally need bathing as they keep themselves clean; but unfortunately, for both cat and owner, sometimes they get in a mess and you will have no choice but to attempt this seemingly im-paw-sible task. It is essential to prepare *before* you inform your cat of what is about to happen. You will need warm water, towels, perhaps a suitable cat shampoo and, whatever you do, keep that bathroom door shut! *See also* ANGER, LICKING

BEDS

Inside cupboards or drawers, nestled among soft toys or laundry, on the sofa or the human bed, cats have a lot of sleeping to do and they like to mix it up. The temptation to shower them with cosy cat igloos or adorable doll beds is strong but getting them to sleep in the new cat bed can be a challenge. Location is very im-paw-tant – it needs to be warm, quiet and purr-haps raised – and sometimes just moving a bed is enough to make them consider your fancy new purchase. You could also try some pheromone spray, catnip or treats to make it more appealing. *See also* CATNIP, PHEROMONES

BEDTIME

Cats are extremely persistent in getting what they want and sleeping with you is probably top of their list. This may or may not work for you – spending the night with your cat can be testing and you may find yourself in a power struggle with a determined feline. They are crepuscular, so they are most active in twilight, which can make them rather pesky at bedtime and early in the morning. Just like children, cats thrive on a bedtime routine and you will all sleep more soundly if you stick to a regular schedule with clear signals. Most cats will settle down at night if they have everything they need: accessible food and water and a nice warm spot, preferably snuggled up with you. Tire young cats out with some play and they are likely to zonk out more easily. *See also* SLEEP, YOWLING

BELLS

Sadly, we are not talking about bells on tiny hats here, though that would be cute, but bells on collars, which can be helpful in thwarting your killer's hunting efforts. However, you will need to change the bell every so often, as the clever little minxes learn to move stealthily without ringing the bell! *See also* ACCESSORIES, BIRDS

Mr Jingles

BELLY RUBS

It's the ultimate sign of trust for your fluffball to expose their belly and it's very tempting to get your hand in all that fur, but beware, as some cats do not like their tummies touched even when they have presented them to you on a plate. Others will lull you into a false sense of security and allow you some affectionate tickles but then the claws and teeth will suddenly come out!

BENGAL

These beautiful miniature leopards were created by crossing the Asian leopard cat with the domestic cat. Earlier generations needed very experienced owners to manage their wilder natures, but contemporary Bengals are said to be better suited to a family home. They are highly active and of superior intelligence and, rather unusually, love to play in water.

BIRDS

It's heart-breaking for cat owners when their cats hunt birds, although only some cats will have the ability to actually catch adult birds. If your cat is one of these, fitting a bell to their collar can significantly reduce the number of victims. You can also limit your cat's chances by keeping them inside an hour before sunset and an hour after sunrise when birds are most busy. Playing frequently with your cat should also reduce their need to hunt outside. *See also* BELLS, FEATHERS, HUNTING

BIRMAN

Thought to originate from Burma, these fluffy, pointed, blue-eyed beauties are said to make gentle and affectionate pets.

BITING

It can surprise new cat owners that gentle biting is one of the many communication methods in your cat's toolbox. Your pussycat may give you a nip on the ankle to get your attention, to show affection, to warn you they've had enough stroking or to protest at being kicked off a warm lap. Kittens will learn not to bite hard during socialization, but there will be moments when play gets over enthusiastic. Make sure you're not being used as a toy and redirect play to a soft toy they can sink their teeth into. Real biting that breaks the skin is a different matter and you need to seek professional help!

BLACK CATS

Who wouldn't want their own small-scale panther? Sleek and sophisticated, black cats are apparently still getting a hard time and take longer to rehome, according to rescue organizations, with grumbles that they are incompatible with the perfect social media shot. However, with the right lighting and a simple background, black cats can shine in all their beauty. It seems black felines are also still associated with bad luck, but we know better; no matter the colour, a cat brings nothing but joy. See also MAGIC, WITCHES

BLEP

When your cute kitty forgets to put their tongue away.
#blep See also TONGUE OUT TUESDAY, SCENT

BLUE EYES

Just like human babies, all kittens are born with blue eyes and their eye colour changes at around six to seven weeks old. Siamese, and some other breeds like Ragdolls and Balinese, hold on to their blue eyes and will use them at every opportunity to seduce you with their bedazzling gaze. It's hard not to forget why you are cross with those sweet blues staring up at you.

BOXES

Guaranteed to make your kitty's day, a new cardboard box of any size or condition is an exciting event in any cat household. Whether it is because the box feels safe and shielding, warm and cosy, or it just needs some thorough investigating, no self-respecting cat can resist climbing straight into a box and trying it out for size. It may amuse you and your pussycat to try the

Endless a-mews-ment

Kanizsa illusion on the floor – cut quarters out of four black circles and place them on the floor to make a square – as many cats are impelled to sit inside the illusory box. *See also* IF I FITS I SITS

BREAKFAST

It's the unspoken rule of every home that the cat gets fed before anyone else. Lie-ins are no longer possible once you have a cat, unless you plan ahead and leave them plenty of dry food the night before. Even then, they will think of some other cat reason to wake you up nice and early. Thanks for that, kitty.

THE CAT LOVER'S A TO Z

BREECHES

Also known as Britches, essentially this refers to extra floof on the back of the hind legs. *See also* FLOOF

BRITISH SHORTHAIR AND LONGHAIR

A popular, solid breed with cute round faces, chubby cheeks and button noses. They descended from the cream of the first domestic cats, and this might explain their independent and laid-back natures.

BUN

Also known as the doughnut or the crescent, the tightly curled bun sleeping position is a neat and tidy way to snooze while keeping warm and cosy. *See also* CROISSANT

BURMILLA

The most popular of the Asian cat group, Burmillas combine the sweet features of a Burmese with the pretty tipped coat and kohl-like lined eyes of a Chinchilla. They are reported to be inquisitive and friendly.

A purr-fectly baked bun

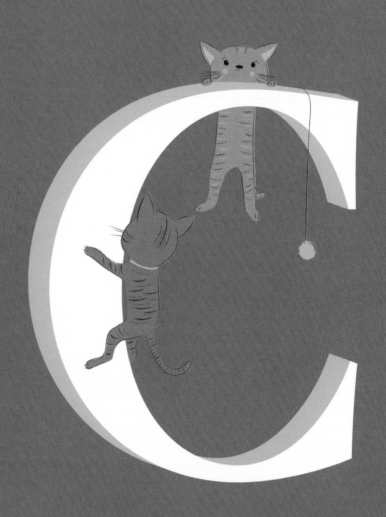

CALICO

Also known as tortoiseshell and white, or chintz, the classic and beloved calico coat has three colours and can be short or longhaired. Whereas the tortoiseshell cat has a black undercoat, calicos are mostly white with prominent patches of black and orange. Calico colouring appears in many breeds and almost all calico cats are female.

CAMEO

A white coat with pretty tips of red, tortoiseshell or cream.

CARNIVORE

Cats are true carnivores and their ideal diet would be small prey such as mice and birds, often eaten in their entirety, crunchy bits and all, but this isn't practical for the modern feline. The first house cats were likely fed meat and fish scraps and leftovers and would probably have eaten most things tossed their way, but today's cats can be very purr-ticular about what they eat. Your cat may bring in prey but not eat it because the food on their plate is scrummier. *See also* FOOD, PREY

An expert at procuring snacks

Not happy

CARRIERS

There is a baffling variety of
different carriers available to
choose from for transporting
your reluctant fuzzy chum
around, from baskets
and cages to flatpacks
and backpacks. Cats are
territorial, so when you take
them out of their territory,
they're never going to be delighted, but
if you choose wisely, you may reap the rewards.
Your cat needs space to move around comfortably, perhaps have a
little stretch and a lie-down, but it also needs to be snug enough to
feel secure. Every cat owner has experienced the unwilling animal
who will resist that carrier with all their might, but if you approach
the operation with military planning, you might have more success.
Treats, pheromone sprays, familiar-smelling blankets and a calming
voice are all advised, but don't expect your stubborn friend to be
easily won over. *See also* VETS

CAT BOX SUNDAY

It's Sunday, so it must be time to capture and share your kitty being
cute in a box; whether sitting neatly in the purr-fect sized container,
or squished elegantly into an unsuitable carton, everyone loves to
see a cat in a box. #catboxsunday *See also* BOXES, CATURDAY,
FLUFFY FURSDAY, IF I FITS I SITS, JELLY BELLY
FRIDAY, KITTY LOAF MONDAY, MEOW MONDAY,
TONGUE OUT TUESDAY, WHISKERS WEDNESDAY

CAT DAD OR CAT MUM

Devoted human parent. Duties will vary wildly, but mostly a food provider and payer of vet bills. *See also* FUR BABY

CATERWAUL

A terrible racket from your feline, with the volume turned up as far as it will go. Even the sweetest of kitties have this shrill yowl in their communication repertoire and it could be a sign of immense displeasure, pain, fear or raging hormones. A complaint level often saved for car journeys, and likely to literally drive you to distraction. *See also* DISPLEASURE, TRAVEL

CAT FANCY

The world of fancy cat breeding and showing, lots of floof guaranteed. *See also* CAT SHOWS, PEDIGREE

CAT FLAP

If you have an outdoor cat, a cat flap is an essential piece of kit. Otherwise, you could remain at the beck and call of your miniature despot and have to open the door every time they want to go out or come in; you can guarantee they will abuse the system and decide it's an excellent game to play with their gullible human. You can get fancy cat flaps with timers and microchip recognition, so if you don't want other cats coming in or want to stop your cat going out all the time, you can infuriate your pet with some rare control over them. Even if they have used a cat flap for years, some cats will approach it tentatively each time, as if it is a strange newfangled object from space, while others will charge through without a moment's hesitation.

CAT LADY

Sometimes MAD CAT LADY or CRAZY CAT LADY, and while it's often meant as a put-down, this is a badge of honour we'd proudly wear. The term is frequently used to refer to single women with cats, whether they are 'old spinsters' or perhaps, younger career-minded women. It can also refer to owners of multiple cats, and the label has been happily adopted by some in the lesbian community.

CATNIP

This herb has magical properties that will instantly transform your sophisti-cat into a giddy, purring, drooling mess. It is thought catnip affects over two-thirds of the house cat population, and even some wild cats go crazy for the plant. The envy-inspiring endorphin hit will give your cat a blissful experience for around ten to fifteen minutes. *See also* TOYS, VALERIAN

Catnip: kitty heaven

CAT SHOWS

Whether you have a moggy or a pedigree, there could be a show for you and your purr-fect partner. If you love cats, shows could be a fun day out to gawp at pretty kitties, find out more about the different breeds and discover all the feline paraphernalia out there. If you want to show your cat off and come home flaunting a cup or rosette, it might be a good idea to start young. While most cats seem to adapt to the show routine, much of the enjoyment is likely to be yours, though some cats seem to enjoy the fuss. Either way, all cats are champs in our eyes. *See also* CAT FANCY, PEDIGREE

CAT SITTERS

Everyone will need to be away at some point in their cat's life and it can be hard to know what to do with our precious friends. The cat sitter, who will visit or even stay in your home, is a modern miracle that your cat will thank you for booking. Whether they decide to turn their nose up and ignore the sitter or enthusiastically roll around at their feet, demanding tummy tickles, most cats will prefer to be in their own territory and you can enjoy your time away knowing your cat is safe and sound at home.

CATTERY

If a cat sitter isn't right for you or your cat, a boarding cattery may be your best option if you are going away. A good cattery will have outside space, climbing and hiding areas and will take the time to find out all about your kitty's unique purr-sonality. However much your cat has been pampered during their stay, be prepared for the cold shoulder on your return. Cats are skilful at sulking but give them a day or two and they might be prepared to move on, if not forgive.
See also CAT SITTERS, DISPLEASURE

CATURDAY

The biggest day of the week in any cat-owning household, this is a chance to share and celebrate our cats' purr-culiar charms. With humans more likely to be at home on a Saturday, cats either love it or hate it, depending on your furry friend's sensibilities.
#caturday *See also* CAT BOX SUNDAY, FLUFFY FURSDAY, JELLY BELLY FRIDAY, KITTY LOAF MONDAY, MEOW MONDAY, TONGUE OUT TUESDAY, WHISKERS WEDNESDAY

*A diet is on the cards
for this chonk*

CHIN
One of the favourite stroking sweet spots for many felines. Rubbing
your fingers along the side of their furry chin is generally very
welcome and has the added bonus of marking you with their scent.

CHINCHILLA
These green-eyed Persian fluffballs have a white undercoat with
black tips that gives them an otherworldly glittery appearance.
Said to thrive with plenty of peace and quiet. *See also* BURMILLA

CHONK
Also known as round, tubby or plump. Although this dictionary is
not here to judge, if you suspect your cat is a little on the chonky
side, a diet or some gentle encouragement to exercise might be
advised. Your cat may disagree but larger cats are more at risk of
health problems, so some tough love may be required. #chonk
See also DIETS, SLONK

CITRUS

A very offensive scent for our delicate friends. Utilize it if you want to keep your cat away from something and they will avoid it like the plague. Or they might not, being the contrary so-and-sos they are. *See also* SMELL, YUCK

CLAWS

You might think the little terrors destroy your furniture to drive you crazy, and while there might be a little truth to this, cats are also masters at self-maintenance and that includes keeping their treasured weapons in tip-top condition. Exercising those claws keeps them trim and removes the outer layer every now and then to reveal shiny new ones beneath, and well-looked after claws means essential defence, good climbing and expert hunting. A scratching post will certainly make your moggy much happier and hopefully keep your furniture safer too. *See also* SCRATCH POST, SOFAS

CLIMBING

One of the most im-paw-tant activities in any feline's day, as all cats have a strong instinct to ascend – they are nice and secure up high, they can survey their territory, it's great exercise and, first and foremost, it's fun. If you have an indoor cat, make sure they have the ability to climb and you'll have a much happier cat. There's a vast array of cat trees and gyms available, but the higher the pole the better. *See also* CLAWS, FALLS, TREES

*Climbing op-paw-tunities
are essential*

COATS

Domestic kitties are generally grouped by longhair, semi-longhair and shorthair. A shorthair coat will need little input from you, but the more hair, the more work for you, with the exception of hairless breeds that need careful cleaning. A healthy cat will have a shiny and smooth coat, a pleasure to stroke, but genetics will ultimately decide the colour, pattern, length and feel of a cat's coat.
See also FUR, GROOMING

COLLARS

While there is something undeniably cute about a cat in a smart collar, you may not need one with the marvel of microchipping. However, you might want to give your cat a collar to make it clear they are not a stray, to attach a bell to, or to put your contact details on for swift communication. Some may require a 'DO NOT FEED ME' tag if they are inclined to visit friends for a snack. Make sure you buy a quick release one in case they get caught on a branch or fence and be prepared for the more mischievous cat to regularly return minus their new collar. *See also* BELLS, NEIGHBOURS

COMMUNICATION

To an outsider, cats can seem a little inscrutable, with their poker-faces and aloof body language, but the feline owner knows better. Once you tune into your cat, you will discover they use their bodies, ears, eyes, tail, voices and rubbing to convey subtle (or not so subtle) meaning. From the discreet but profound slow blink to the slightest twitch of the tail, our kitties have a whole repertoire at their disposal to communicate with us, other cats and the world outside, much of it invisible to us. *See also* DISPLEASURE, LANGUAGE

*The cone of shame
is misery for all*

CONE OF SHAME

The most dreaded of all things, the cumbersome Elizabethan collar will traumatize everyone in the household, but sometimes there is no alternative to stop your kitty licking and interfering with their wounds. The days will pass miserably at a snail's pace and your troubled puss may make a concerted effort to remove it, cry incessantly or quietly brood, plotting their revenge, but whichever route they choose, it will break your heart. New alternatives to consider include inflatable doughnuts and body suits, but always check with your vet. *See also* NEUTERING

CORNISH REX

An intelligent and energetic shorthaired breed with a very fine, wavy coat and large distinctive ears. Not a cat to leave alone all day.

COURTSHIP

Generally female cats give male cats a wide berth, but it's a different matter when it comes to mating. Most female cats are ready to mate by around six months, but shockingly they can get pregnant as young as four months, so you need to move swiftly to avoid an unplanned wooing. You should aim to have your kitten neutered before they hit puberty, otherwise your little lady will become obsessed with hooking up with a suitable tomcat and will make everyone's life hell. When she's ready to mate, your female puss will tell you and the whole neighbourhood all about it and she'll start rolling around, purring and kneading everything in sight. She will soon attract the local lads, who will lie in wait for an opportunity with your irresistible lady. *See also* MATING CALL, NEUTERING

CREPUSCULAR

Our feline friends are most active during twilight and their eyes are well-adapted to hunt during these hours. Your pussycat can be really quite annoying when you are at your most tired, particularly if you have an indoor cat or keep your cat in during these hours to avoid unwanted gifts. Help  them to follow their instincts with an energetic play session and get it out of their system before bedtime. We doubt there are many owners who will get up especially for this chore, so pulling your duvet over your head is probably your best option in the early hours. *See also* ZOOMIES

CROISSANT

Arguably the most popular of feline sleeping positions, the classic croissant is a slightly open bun with paws visible. Some cats a-paw-rently enjoy a nibble on a real croissant too. *See also* BUN

The croissant

CUDDLES

We've all tried to pick up a cat only to find they have firmly dug their claws into the ground or the nearest object and will not budge. It's an embarrassing situation for you both and will only end well if you backtrack. The compulsion to pick up and cuddle our fur babies is hard to ignore but some cats will not thank you for it. Look for signs your feline is in the mood, such as an upright tail and friendly rubbing before attempting a lift. If you put a cat down quickly if they're not enjoying it, they will learn to trust you. Some pliable pusses will enjoy being held like a baby, some love to sit on a shoulder or snuggle in your arms, while others will find the intensity of a cuddle too much to handle. Learn what your cat purr-ticularly likes, and you will both be happier. *See also* CHIN, LAP CAT, STROKES

CURIOSITY

It killed the cat. There is no doubt cats are incredibly curious and will stick their snooping noses into most things. This ceaseless interest in life is what makes them so charming, but a-paw-rently this well-known saying may have originally meant 'worry will kill the cat'. Whether anxious or curious, luckily neither is likely to actually kill your cat, but just like humans, stress can impact their health, so be mindful of their sensitive natures.
See also ANXIETY, INSPECTION

DAM

Not 'that damn cat!' – though arguably that should have its own entry – but dam here means the female parent.

DECORATIONS

Everything and anything in your home is a potential toy for your fluffy pal and they will welcome the addition of your delicate new decorations with open claws. Paper garlands will be shredded within minutes, bunting torn down and paper fans kicked into submission. Christmas trees are purr-ticularly exciting and any self-respecting feline will have to attempt an expedition to the summit. Avoid glass decorations and tinsel and be prepared for much festive chaos.

Festive decoration chaos

DENIM

Cats can be very purr-ticular about the clothing of their humans and some may not appreciate the roughness of denim when selecting a lap for a snooze, while others will find the scratch-ability irresistible. Jeans are often strewn on chairs and smell of us, so you may find your cat loves to snuggle down in them.

*Devilish behaviour is to be expected
but costumes are not appreciated*

DEVIL

The cats of medieval Europe were frequently associated with the devil himself and suffered because of it. Every cat has more than a little devilish behaviour in them, and that's why we love them, but luckily those days of being misunderstood are mostly behind them. *See also* BLACK CATS, GODS & GODDESSES, VILLAINS, WITCHES

DEVON REX

A breed similar in appearance to their neighbours, the Cornish Rex, with sparse wavy coats and sizeable ears. Known for their playful and characterful personalities. *See also* CORNISH REX, SPHYNX

DIETS

There may come a time in your cat's life, often in middle age, when your vet will gently point out your cat's expanding waistline. While you may appreciate your extra-cuddly puss, you are doing their health no favours. Embarking on a diet is no mean feat but with your vet's advice, you should try to find a food and activity regime to shed those extra pounds. Biscuits are quite calorie dense, and reducing these a little can be a good place to start; weigh their food too, but remember that some manufacturers may advise more than necessary. You may have to feed your cats separately if one is dining out on several bowls, or consider a 'DO NOT FEED ME' tag for those cheeky fluffballs begging from your well-meaning

neighbours or stealing from the local cats. Your cat will certainly protest but will ultimately thank you for their new-found energy and slinky waists. It's difficult to get them to shed excess weight so keep an eye on your cat's diet – prevention is better than cure!
See also CHONK, FOOD

DISCIPLINE

Don't even think about it – cats will not respond well to discipline and it could damage your relationship with your best fur-iend. Never use physical domination of your cat or shout at it even though this can be hard when they're pushing their luck. Instead, reward and praise when they are doing well and ignore or divert any bad behaviour and your cat will quickly learn. Cats are not as impervious to your feelings as they can sometimes seem.
See also ANGER, MISDEEDS

DISHWASHER

Cats can be weirdos and your feline may be unmoved by this appliance, fear it like a monster or be captivated by it. Some cats, and especially kittens, will leap into the dishwasher at any opportunity, tiptoeing through treacherous spikes and mucky plates, and position themselves, impossible to reach, at the back. They will smugly gaze at you, safe in their new lair. Other cats will enjoy the soothing noise, warmth and vibrations and will choose to nap on top of them. A superior hiding spot is to be found underneath the open dishwasher door, so make sure you don't squish your lurking feline.

Discipline will fall on deaf ears

DISPLEASURE

Cats are expert at communicating their feelings and whether it's a disdainful look, a swipe of the paw or the cold shoulder, make no mistake, you will know when your cat is displeased with you.
See also CATTERY, CUDDLES, DIETS

DOGS

You might be a cat person *and* a dog person and want both species of fur baby in your life. Popular culture tells us cats and dogs can't be friends and indeed their natural instincts would keep them apart. However, many households have both and, if not always perfectly harmonious, they can generally learn to get along. They might end up the best of fur-iends and enjoy endless playfighting and naps curled up together, or they may peacefully agree to give each other a wide berth. Of course, they may also drive each other up the wall and cause you endless headaches. Depending on their breed, background and upbringing, some pairings will work better, so do your research beforehand to avoid trouble.

DOORS

Cats really do not like shut doors. Ever. Go to the bathroom and your cat will soon be outside miaowing to get in. Close your office door for some peace and they'll be scratching underneath. Open the back door for your pestering puss and they will quickly be fussing to get back in. Cats need access to ALL their territory at ALL times and remember that they will *always* win. *See also* CURIOSITY, OUTDOORS

A closed door is always a cat-astrophe

DOZING

A cat's full-time job. Around three quarters of a cat's daily sleep quota is dedicated to dozing. While in snooze mode, your pussycat can still smell and hear and can snap into action at a moment's notice. Waft those treats under their nose and they will soon know about it. *See also* BEDS, NAPS, SLEEP

DRAWERS

The more intelligent feline will easily master the art of opening drawers and this enthralling game will probably involve emptying said drawers of all their contents. Each cat will find their own idiosyncratic method of accessing your undies and while heavy wooden drawers or child locks may solve the issue, redirecting their interest swiftly with a favourite toy kept nearby may distract them from their task.

A thorough drawer inspection

DREAMS

Rather adorably, it seems very likely that cats have dreams too. With the cutest kneading paws, twitching whiskers and indecipherable mumbles, your kitty is probably processing their busy day during their REM sleep, just as we do.

EARS

Cat ears are little wonders of engineering and are arguably their most recognizable and cutest feature. Feline hearing is superior to both humans and dogs and an impressive thirty-two ear muscles allow cats to rotate their ears towards a sound and move each one individually. Their ears are also an im-paw-tant way to communicate, from the classic flattened ears to the slightest twist at the sound of their name, so do pay attention.

ELEGANT

Even the daffiest of cats has an innate elegance, from the graceful sashay of their walk to their polished appearance. You may question this when your cat is licking their bottom or enthusiastically attacking a smelly shoe, but look carefully and you will see even these inelegant tasks are performed with a classiness we can all aspire to.

EUROPEAN SHORTHAIR

A less stocky version of the British and American Shorthairs which are popular in Scandinavia, these independent-spirited cats are adaptable and playful.

EYES

We tend to assume our feline friends see the world, through those exquisite eyes, as we do. However, cats are not very good at seeing objects up close to them or far away as they are mid-sighted, so sometimes will struggle to see the toy or treat you have presented before them. They can detect movement extremely quickly and have good sight in dim light, all purr-fect attributes for hunting. They also see colour differently from us and everything appears with a softly muted filter. How very tasteful! *See also* BLUE EYES, STARING

FALLS

In the wild, cats spend a lot of time in trees, but even the most sure-footed felines are prone to the odd mistake and a snoozing or distracted cat may find themselves plummeting down to earth. Luckily our skilful cats have a righting reflex that swiftly kicks into action and allows them to land purr-fectly. However, falling from more than one storey can be more dangerous and cats falling from windows and balconies can sustain nasty injuries, so be sure to keep windows closed or screened. Amazingly, there are records of cats surviving eye-wateringly-high falls almost unscathed, and this can a-paw-rently be explained by mind-boggling physics and physiology.
See also CLIMBING, TREES

Heading for the purr-fect landing

FAVOURITES

Playing favourites as a pet owner is strictly forbidden, but cats seem to be exempt and often favour one person in the household. It can be frustrating if you are not their number one human and rather trying if you are the constant target of their affections. One study revealed that cats simply gravitate to the person who makes the most effort to get to know them, so taking the time to read their body language, learn their likes and dislikes and playing with them could help matters. However, your cat's temperament could also be key – if they like peace and quiet, they will probably favour the laid-back member of the family.

FEAR

Some timid cats will flee at the slightest thing. Like humans, some are just wired this way or they may have had a difficult start in life. If your cat keeps hiding under the bed, leave them be until they calm down and try to resist enticing them out. It can be hard to leave your furball alone, but let a shy cat approach you when it's ready and keep to a predictable routine to build their confidence. Pheromone sprays and a relaxed demeanour can also help. Some faint-hearted cats will find a toy hard to resist and you can bond this way. A big change in your cat's purr-sonality should be checked out with a vet.
See also ANXIETY, FIGHTING

FEATHERS

Hopefully your cat is not getting much opportunity to get hold of the genuine article, so they will appreciate the dazzling array of feather wands, teasers and wagglers, available for their amusement. The right feather toy will bring out the kitten in even the most jaded of sourpusses. See also BIRDS, PLAY, TOYS

Feather fun without the murder

*Affection comes by the
bucket load at feeding time*

FEEDING TIME

For most cats, it is time to engage in some assiduous leg weaving
and encouraging meows to ensure you do not forget the im-paw-
tant task at hand. It is a nice way to bond with your kitty. Most
like to have small, frequent meals over the course of the day and
some will graze all day while others will scoff the whole lot in one
go. Most cat owners divide their meals into at least two a day, but
many feed their cat when they ask, if they are at home with them.
Be careful with this method or you might end up with a chonk.
Avoid squabbles between cats with a bowl each placed apart.
See also CHONK, FOOD, LEG RUBBING

FELIS CATUS

A suitably fancy, scientific name for the humble house cat, a member
of the magnificent Felidae cat family. Fittingly, it sounds like a Roman
em-purr-or or em-purr-ess.

Fisticuffs is generally to be avoided

FIGHTING

You may have squabbling siblings or a cat that gets into scraps with the neighbourhood toms, but unless you have a solitary indoor cat, you are unlikely to avoid a clash at some point. Cats will fight and it can be alarming to see your beloved puss in a heated boxing match, but keep calm if you can! Don't stride in and risk a clawing, but make a loud noise or, if you feel you need to intervene, arm yourself with a thick blanket. Make sure your cats aren't competing for resources and supply them with their own food bowls, water, litter trays and plenty of places to safely rest without ambush. They may be playfighting and, as long as it is reciprocal and neither is getting hurt, it can be great fun for the cats. Cats in the outside world will generally prefer to avoid confrontation and, rather cleverly, can get to know each other's routines and be able to avoid each other, but the odd stand-off is inevitable. *See also* ANGER, QUARRELS, TOMCAT

FIREWORKS

Some cats won't bat an eyelid but others find fireworks stressful, so keep them inside, shut the blinds and put the TV on for background noise. If you exude calm, hopefully your cat will follow your lead, but leave them in peace if they want to hide until they feel it is safe to come out.

FISH

Cats traditionally hate getting wet, but when it comes to two of their favourite pastimes – fun and food – they might be willing to put a paw in the water. They love to gaze at ponds and aquariums and will not hesitate to try and catch a fish if an opportunity presents itself. Some cats go crazy for the taste of fish, but it doesn't fulfil all their nutritional needs so reserve it for an occasional yummy snack or treat. *See also* AQUARIUM, TUNA

FLEAS

Once a month you will learn to sneak up like a ninja on your unsuspecting puss and apply a deeply offensive liquid to the back of their neck. Your bewildered kitty will not understand why you would do such a thing and will make their feelings clear. There are also small and tasty tablets available from the vet, which will do the trick if the liquid is a no-go with your cat. Fingers crossed, you shouldn't encounter too many problems with fleas if you apply this treatment with regularity, but if you do lose control, talk to your vet, as you will need a sophisticated plan to treat both your home and pet. Look out for bites on your ankles and an irritable, scratching cat, purr-ticularly over the summer months. *See also* DISPLEASURE

FLOOF

An abundance of fluff. #floof

A floofball

FLUFFY FURSDAY

Thursday has come around and it is time to break out those snaps of your puss in all their fluffy glory. Furry chests, chubby cheeks and fuzzy tummies especially welcome. #fluffyfursday *See also* CATURDAY, CAT BOX SUNDAY, JELLY BELLY FRIDAY

FOOD

Cats can be fusspots and will generally end up getting what they want. Some cats love wet food and others prefer dry, while a combination of the two can be the purr-fect compromise. Dry food varies a great deal in size and content, so shop around for the right match for your puss. It may not seem that exciting to us, but as long as you choose a well-balanced dry food, it may be all your cat needs and wants, but make sure they have enough water to drink. An occasional morsel of cooked lean meat, egg or fish from the human table can be a nice treat, but be sure to avoid onion and garlic. Introducing different types of wet and dry food, with a variety of textures and flavours, from an early age helps to avoid a picky eater. *See also* CHONK, FEEDING TIME, TREATS, WET FOOD

FRIENDS

Felines are solitary but social creatures and you might be lucky enough to have some BFFs in your home. Some cats are so well bonded they'll sleep cuddled up and groom each other but, alas, even bringing up kittens together doesn't guarantee domestic bliss when they grow up. Introduce new cats to each other slowly – starting with their scent – and they are more likely to accept each other.

Fur-ever best fur-iends

FROGS

Anyone who has ever had a live frog brought into their bedroom will confirm cats really love to chase our little green friends. Keeping your cat inside at dusk will reduce their opportunities to torment them and save the frogs, and you, some trauma. Until you get a cat, most people don't realize that frogs can scream like a banshee. *See also* GIFTS, HUNTING

FUR

You can guarantee your furry pal will make a bee line for you if you have made an effort to dress up and will swiftly cover your chic black outfit in their fluff. Even the most aloof cat will bring out their best cunning moves to swamp you in fur on your way out. There are three types of hair in a cat's coat – a fluffy down to keep them toasty, the most visible layer of awn hair and outer guard hairs to keep them dry. When the temperature goes up, cats will shed their thick winter coats and you'll be covered in the stuff. Lint rollers and hand-held vacuums are recommended.

FUR BABY

The apple of your eye. #furbaby *See also* JOY

FURBALLS

These delightful hairballs are dramatically thrown up by your feline every once in a while, and are often mixed with grass for extra wow. More common in longhaired cats and generally nothing to fear, but if you have a repeat offender on your hands, there are special diets available to help. Also doubles up as another cute name for felines. *See also* GRASS

GARDEN

If you have a garden, however small, and your cat goes outside, it is likely this space will form a part of your cat's territory. Cats love the stimulation of the outside environment and you can make your garden particularly appealing with a nice spot to lie in the sun, shrubs to hide in, catnip to enjoy and plenty of climbing and scratching opportunities. Keep the birds safe with feeders on high poles.
See also HEDGEWATCH

GARLIC

Eating garlic and onions is harmful to our pussycats, so don't let them nibble on your garlic chicken leftovers, though they are likely to turn their noses up anyway. A-paw-rently planting garlic in the garden is likely to ward off felines and, scandalously, there are even recipes for homemade cat-repelling garlic sprays!

GHOSTS

Whether it's the ultimate cat prank, or they really are sensing an eerie presence, cats take great pleasure in reacting to absolutely nothing, ideally when you are on your own in the house, to give you the shudders. They may stare intently at a spot in the room, ears pricked and whiskers twitching, or they may go the whole hog and bring out the low growl and tensed body to really put the wind up you.

Spooked

A more acceptable gift

GIFTS

Your furry friend may proudly bring you a macabre present from time to time and it can be hard to suppress your horror if you have not employed them for their superior mouser skills. Try not to freak out, but calmly and kindly remove and safely dispose of the kill at the first opportunity. They are following their instincts and will be perplexed by your anger if you scold them. Cats are unfortunately killing machines but you can reduce their kill rate substantially with bells, food with a high protein content, lots of vigorous play and a curfew. Rather cutely, some cats (perhaps less successful at hunting) will bring home much more welcome random objects like leaves and sticks for you too! *See also* BELLS, BIRDS, CARNIVORE, HUNTING

GINGER

These iconic marmalade felines are beloved the world over. Most likely to be male, only one in five are female. Orange cats are described as red in the fancier world of cat breeding and all have tabby markings, where red pigment replaces the black or brown pigment, whether it is clearly visible or very faint. Many breeds have ginger varieties, from the floofy red Persian to the slinky red point Siamese.

Rightly worshipped throughout history

GODS & GODDESSES

If you invite a cat into your home, you will soon be worshipping at their velvety feet. Our little deities undoubtedly have a confidence and wisdom that marks them out as superior beings in our eyes. The ancient Egyptians appreciated the mystical qualities of our favourite housemates, and while perhaps not seen as gods themselves, they were certainly revered and thought to bring good fortune. Today's cat bow-ties and crystal-studded collars might seem a new trend, but wealthy Egyptians are thought to have dressed their beloved pets in jewels and lavished them with treats too! *See also* RELIGION

GRASS

You will often see a cat happily munching on a patch of grass and it is a clever means of bringing up those pesky hairballs. If you have an indoor cat, they will benefit from a pot of grass to chomp on. *See also* FURBALLS

GRIMALKIN

A not especially flattering name for a cat, sometimes an older, female cat, it literally means 'grey cat', although it is associated with a witch's familiar. All of our furry friends have days when we might want to call them this.

GROCERIES

It's pretty exciting when you come home with bags of new scrunchy items and your kitty will love to get inside and have a snoop around. Ideally all items will be given a quick sniff and a rub before they are whisked away. For some reason, our weird pals also seem to like sitting on plastic bags – maybe they like the feel or the exciting rustle – and might even have a chew, so make sure you don't leave them lying around.

Im-paw-tant grocery inspection

*Grooming is a
fur-avourite pastime*

GROOMING

A favourite feline pastime, cats will spend hours preening to keep
their coats in tip-top condition. Dare to interrupt this protracted
ritual and your cat will pause and throw you a suitably displeased
glance before returning to the serious task at hand. Many kitties don't
need any help with grooming at all; however, if you have a floofball
or a cat that can't groom itself, you will need to equip yourself with
some kit for a daily brushing. It's best to start this process young
and it can be a lovely way to bond with your puss. Even those that
look after themselves may occasionally come home with something
unsightly marring their beautiful coats and need a little assistance –
but they probably won't thank you.

GROWLING

This deep and prolonged rumbling sound tells you your feline means
business. It is a serious warning to a human or challenger that they
are not to be messed with.

HAPPINESS

We can learn a great deal about purr-fect happiness from our fluffy chums. Cats are masters at enjoying the moment and will take the time to appreciate the small pleasures in life, such as feeling the warmth of the sun on their coats or the tickle of your fingers on their furry cheek. They exude a quiet pleasure, from their gently closed, smiling eyes to their laid-back posture and satisfied purrs.

HEAT

Held in high regard and highly sought-after by any feline, whether it's a tiny patch of sunshine on the rug, a prized position in front of the fire or a place on your cosy lap, cats are dedicated to seeking out the warm spots in your home and will stop at nothing to claim them. Even a knobbly radiator will not deter our heat-loving kitties, so try a heated pad or a radiator bed and they'll love you fur-ever. *See also* NAPS

Radiator bliss

HEDGEWATCH

Any feline will want to include some hedgewatching in their day. Whether from a window or out on paw-trol, many an hour can be whiled away observing the wonders of the natural world from a safe post. Cold starts to the day have been known to delay this im-paw-tant work. #hedgewatch *See also* GARDEN, PATROL

Hiding: can be hazardous

HIDING

Cats are geniuses at hiding and you will find them in the most curious places – they might be on top of the wardrobe, curled up in a drawer, squeezed inside a laundry basket or under the dishwasher door. Our feline friends just love to hide, whether it's to have a peaceful snooze, to get away from something scary or to engage you in play. Your cat might stealthily lie in wait behind a bush or the couch, ready to pounce on you or their housemates. Some pusses can get rather over-enthusiastic when they launch their attack. *See also* HUNTING

HIMALAYAN

Also known as a Colourpoint Persian, these pretty fluffballs have the sparkling blue eyes and points of a Siamese, in a variety of colours. Likely to have more cat-titude from their Siamese lineage than a Persian. *See also* PERSIAN, SIAMESE

HISSING

Hopefully your pet won't be prone to hissy fits, but all cats will occasionally hiss, if not at you then certainly at other cats. Like the low growl, it is an unmistakeably serious warning to pull back. It can be used more gently, as mother cats also hiss at their kittens, and cats in pain may hiss too. *See also* GROWLING

HUNTING

It can be hard to align our goofy pets with the formidable, some might say merciless, hunters they are. Humans began their special relationship with cats *because* of their innate pest-controlling ability and now, for many cat owners, this has become their least appreciated attribute. All that sleeping allows them to preserve enough energy to follow their powerful instincts, and all the playing hones their skills to purr-fection. However, some cats are not as adept as others in their pursuit of prey and you may be lucky enough to have a puss that doesn't bring home the bacon. Plenty of play can keep their instincts at bay and keeping them in at dawn and dusk will help reduce their opportunities. *See also* BIRDS, FROGS, MICE, PREY

The hunting instinct is fur real

Our icons of the meow-ment

ICONS

Felines have always enjoyed iconic status and have sparked our imaginations in folk tales, legends, myths, fiction and art. Now they have taken over the internet and much of our time online is spent cooing over the cutest, silliest, weirdest and most superior of cats. Some individual cats are world famous and adored by millions. Cats have definitely won the internet and gained their rightful place at the top of our world. #catoftheday, #catlife, #catlover *See also* GODS & GODDESSES

IDIOCY

Yes, unbelievably, our classy, intelligent and stylish pets can surprise us with their idiocy at times. From getting stuck in an awkward spot to a misjudged pounce or an ungainly slip, our cats can sometimes be ridiculously daft. Even though *we all know* it happened, getting them to *admit* to any of this is frankly im-paws-ible. *See also* SAVING FACE

This seems to be a good fit

IF I FITS I SITS

The sight of a box or bag or gap or hole is an instant challenge to get inside and have a nice sit down; the smaller and more unsuitable, the better. Can also be applied to the feline version of a pile-on, involving multiple cats elegantly squeezed into an area of limited dimensions. Celebrate these wonders of nature online. #ififitsisits *See also* BOXES

ILLNESS

Thankfully our feline friends are pretty healthy creatures, but of course they are not immune to illness and there is nothing worse than seeing your ball of fluff feeling down. Cats are great at concealing illness and will often carry on as normal, but signs there is something wrong include hiding, eating less, sleeping more, drinking lots or less, losing weight and showing aggression. Obviously, see your vet if your cat is ill, but there are things you can do at home to comfort them. Ideally designate a nice warm room for their care away from the hustle and bustle, and set it up with a cosy bed, a litter tray, food and water. However worried you are feeling, try to stay calm, as your cat will detect your anxiety.

IMPERVIOUSNESS

Cats are highly skilled at appearing impervious, and you will find yourself performing like a desperate court jester trying to a-mews them, to elicit a smile, while they gaze at you with suitable disdain or look the other way. Sometimes they are just not in the mood.

IMPULSIVE

Because cats can be hard to read at times, occasionally it feels as if their behaviour comes out of the blue. The cats which appear most impulsive are those with bundles of energy who have never lost their kitten-y *joie de vivre*. Cats are adapted to conserve energy for sudden bursts of action when hunting and they have bullet-fast reactions. If there are opportunities for fun, they'll generally make the most of them and we could all learn from the feline ability to transition from catnap to play in an instant. *See also* INSANITY, ZOOMIES

INDOOR

Cats love to roam and investigate the natural world but you may need to keep your cat indoors for a variety of reasons, and there is plenty you can do to keep your pet as happy and healthy as possible. Cat food puzzles are a great way to keep them challenged throughout the day, while opportunities to climb and explore are essential. Your puss will also need plenty of stimulation, from safe plants to interact with, to the feel of fresh air in their fur, and a revolving selection of interesting toys. Also consider a catio, enclosed garden or walks on a lead to keep life invigorating. *See also* CLIMBING, LEADS

Hopefully a view is paw-sible

INSANITY

Even the most sophisticated of cats will have some purr-culiar moments, tearing around the place with a mad look in their eye. Your kitty probably hasn't gone crazy but it is likely the release of oodles of bottled up energy from all that daytime napping. If your cat isn't in danger of harming itself or any others that come in its path, sit back and enjoy the chaos. If it's getting out of control, make sure your cat is getting enough exercise and play, check for those bothersome fleas and talk to your vet. *See also* ZOOMIES

INSECTS

An irresistible source of a-mews-ment for any indoor or outdoor puss, insects are guaranteed to keep your cat busy for some hours, with mixed results. Unfortunately for the cat, some insects will retaliate, so be warned.

Beware the stingers

Border police inspection

INSPECTION

Cats are excellent detectives and nothing gets past them without a thorough investigation. They would make amazing border police, although unfortunately couldn't be trusted not to snaffle anything tasty for themselves. They will quickly detect any cases of infidelity, so watch out if you've been snuggling with someone else's kitty.
See also BOXES, GROCERIES, HEDGEWATCH

INTELLIGENCE

Our BFFs are so intelligent they won't even lower themselves to humour scientists, so while the data may be limited, anyone that has ever lived with a cat knows they can outsmart both us and our dogs. Our pocket geniuses understand exactly what we want but choose whether they act on it or not. If you eagerly pat your lap, they may appear to faintly nod, but will often decline the invitation regardless. They operate on a higher plane, they are simply superior to us all and we accordingly worship them for it. They have negotiated the ultimate deal – they get fed, watered and adored but they are also (mostly) free to come and go as they purr-lease.

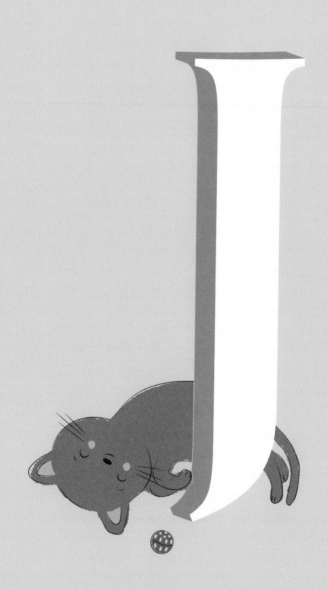

JAWS

If you've ever seen a cat yawn, which they do frequently and rather theatrically, you'll know that they can open their jaws very wide indeed. Our more sensitive readers won't wish to know that this allows them to comfortably bite their prey around the neck.
See also YAWN

JELLY BELLY FRIDAY

Head into the weekend with a chance to marvel at those enticing furry tummies displayed for our delight. A true sign of a happy cat. #jellybellyfriday *See also* CATURDAY, CAT BOX SUNDAY, FLUFFY FURSDAY, KITTY LOAF MONDAY, MEOW MONDAY, TONGUE OUT TUESDAY, WHISKERS WEDNESDAY

JOY

Most cat owners will agree that our furry friends bring us joy by the bucket load. From their ability to soak up our worries to their daft antics and calming purrs, cats brighten our days and soothe our souls. Yes, they can be grumpy and disdainful, but incredibly that makes us laugh too.

JUMPING

From their enormous leaps to the tops of wardrobes to the cutest little hops to nudge our faces, cats love to jump. They can reach impressive heights with precision and ease and even the smallest spring from a sofa is approached with grace. Of course, they will also use their jumping skills on you and will take great pleasure in bouncing on top of you in the middle of the night and giving you the fright of your life.

KICKING

Every cat enjoys a vigorous session kicking the stuffing out of their toys. This instinctive manoeuvre involves their front paws firmly gripping the unlucky victim, while the back legs will furiously thrash away. Just make sure it's not your hand that is the target.

KITTENS

Don't underestimate the menace of these tiny creatures. They will run rings around you and anyone or anything that comes into their path. Their appetites will bankrupt you, their boundless energy will exhaust you and their devious ways will astound you. Be prepared for a wild ride and don't underestimate the attention they will need. Shelters are often inundated with kittens in the summer, so it's a good time to seek out a tiny floofball needing a home. *See also* ADOPTION

KITTY LOAF MONDAY

When your cat tucks their front paws under their body and sits neatly on the floor, they resemble the purr-fect rounded form of a loaf of bread. This is the day to share your freshly baked kitty loaves. #kittyloafmonday *See also* CATURDAY, CAT BOX SUNDAY, FLUFFY FURSDAY, JELLY BELLY FRIDAY, MEOW MONDAY, TONGUE OUT TUESDAY, WHISKERS WEDNESDAY

KNEADING

You will hopefully experience this adorable sign of true contentment. Kittens will busily knead their mother's tummies to get milk, and adult cats often enjoy a good knead on your lap. Most cat lovers will put up with the sharp claws to bond with their blissful felines and some cats like to knead on a soft blanket.

LANGUAGE

You will probably find yourself chatting regularly to your cat and they have a purr-culiar talent for making us feel understood. Most feline owners will vocally greet their cats and explain in great detail where they are going when they leave and when their cat can expect them back. Deciphering the chat from your puss can be more challenging as we are not so well versed in cat speak, but most cats and humans will learn to understand each other purr-fectly well during their time together. *See also* COMMUNICATION

LAP CAT

It is one of life's great pleasures to have a cat sit on your lap. Some cats will hop on you at every opportunity, while others are very particular and will choose your lap only if the conditions are purr-fect and will inspect all laps before selecting the most suitable. A cosy blanket to snuggle under can entice some reluctant furballs. Cats are very contrary and will choose the most inopportune moments to deposit themselves on your lap and you must delay all plans if this occurs. Any other household members will have to wait on you hand and foot, as the slightest movement can ruin the whole thing for a finickety puss and under no circumstances may you use the bathroom.

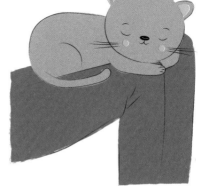

Lap cat:
do not disturb

LAPERM

A Rex breed that lives up to their name and looks as if they have indeed had a perm, with a coat of curls and ringlets. Often self-assured and affectionate, loving heaps of cuddles and attention.

LASERS

Some cats will go wild for these exasperating red dots, and the darting movements will speedily ignite their chasing instincts, but it can get frustrating for your puss, because they never win, they never catch their prey. If your cat enjoys lasers, just make sure they have other toys to dismember and maim during a play session and limit their use. *See also* TOYS

Maddening laser fun

LEADS

Yes astonishingly, it is not so rare now to encounter a feline with a harness, and while a few cats will tolerate it, most will not, because they like to feel in control. If a cat is frightened in an unfamiliar environment they will find it very stressful to be restrained by a lead. Harnesses can be useful for introducing kittens to outside spaces but they will soon want to push the boundaries. For some owners it is a necessary step to provide their pet with some outdoor experiences and every cat is individual in what they can cope with.

Leg rubbing: a fast track to food

LEG RUBBING

Also known as leg weaving, the sweetest greeting after a long day. Your cat may come and affectionately wind between your legs while rubbing their furry faces on you, and this fuzzy reassurance is frequently used to support you while you are cooking your dinner or preparing their food. *See also* FEEDING TIME

Don't stroke during licking or you'll get 'the look'

LICKING

Cats will spend a great deal of time assiduously licking their coats and those of their besties. Often after a pleasing nap, your cat will begin the lengthy task of cleaning their fur from paws to bottom, and they won't thank you for sullying their fur after this procedure. Licking also keeps their fur shiny and watertight, and is a way to cool their body in summer and to bond with their pals, feline or human. Unfortunately, a cat's tongue can be as coarse as a sailor's prose and this honour is not always appreciated.

A private litter tray moment

LITTER TRAY

Much like cat beds and food, cat loo paraphernalia comes in a bewildering range of options. If you remember that your cat is a private animal at their most vulnerable when going to the toilet and will appreciate a safe, quiet space away from an admiring audience, you should be able to find the right kit for your kitty. Your cat will not grant you the same consideration and may well harass and torment you in *your* bathroom. As we also know, cats can be fusspots, so getting the right combination of tray and litter can be a frustrating process.

A purr-fectly baked loaf

LOAF

Whether lazing around in the house or forming the purr-fect bread shape, cats were born to loaf. Our floofy pals are always busy doing nothing and we'd be wise to follow their lead. *See also* KITTY LOAF MONDAY

LONGHAIRED

Their flowing locks may charm the socks off you, and if a lot of floof is your thing, a longhaired cat may be the choice for you. However, purr-ticularly if you choose a pedigree fluffball, be aware they will need a lengthy daily grooming and you may not have a cat that thanks you for it. Remember that all that floof is going to end up all over your home too, and matted fur will need a visit to the vet. *See also* GROOMING, PERSIAN

Hopefully not lost for long

LOST
It's very common for cats to get lost, so try to stay calm. They can vanish for days and return in tip-top shape as if nothing has happened. However, there is no denying the worry of a missing cat and many an owner has lost sleep over their absent felines. Give your home and garden a good once over, then talk to neighbours and check sheds and garages. Use social media and alert local vets, shelters and your microchip register. Leave some familiar smells outside – some of their litter, perhaps some worn clothes or a blanket – and hopefully your puss will be home before you know it. *See also* ALL-NIGHTERS, HIDING

LOUD NOISES
These will be frowned upon by most cats. This includes doorbells, vacuum cleaners, small children, food mixers, loud mew-sic, telephones, chairs scraping, doors slamming, fireworks and yelling. Spare a thought for our sensitive friends the next time you're whizzing up a smoothie. *See also* EARS, MEWSIC

LOVE
We love our cats and we *know* our cats love us. We don't care what anyone else says. End of discussion. *See also* NOSE-BOOP, SLOW BLINK

MACKEREL

Mackerel makes a yummy occasional treat, and there is even a tabby pattern named after it. The striped mackerel tabby can glory in its status as the first, and therefore perhaps the most im-paw-tant, cat. *See also* FISH, TABBY, TUNA

MAGIC

Cats are clearly magic. They can vanish, defy gravity, detect ghosts, see deep into our souls and switch from angel to devil in the blink of an eye. They also hang out with witches, so… *See also* FALLS, GHOSTS, HIDING, WITCHES

MAINE COON

If you like your cats big and floofy, this could be the breed for you. These mighty pusses have impressive swishy tails, tufty ears and big round eyes. They love the great outdoors.

MANES

We are not referring to the lion's mane accessory you wouldn't dare dishonour your cat with, but some breeds, and moggies, already come with majestic manes, including the Maine Coon and Siberian. *See also* ACCESSORIES

MANX

These tailless cats from the Isle of Man come in an a-mews-ingly named range of varieties – including the rumpy (no tail), the stumpy (a short tail) and the longy (you get the picture). They have pleasingly thick fur and a stocky physique.

A 'rumpy' Manx

*Mating calls will delight
the neighbours*

MATING CALL

This bizarre warbling combines all the sounds
at a female's disposal, with a delightful revolving
mix of meows, howls, purrs and trills. Drives
the male tomcats crazy and unfortunately has
the same effect on their owners and neighbours.
Sweet mew-sic for the right pair of tufty ears.
See also COURTSHIP, MEWSIC

MEDITATION

Cats are always just one slow
blink away from a deep meditation.
They spend a great deal of their day
contemplating nothing much at all.
Meditation teachers invite us to join our felines in their tranquil
moments, perhaps stare out of the window for a while with your
cat or find a nice spot in the sun to sit serenely with them. Our
little enlightened friends can help us find inner peace and learn to
appreciate every meow-ment. *See also* WISDOM, YOGA

*Meditative contemplation
or a sneaky doze, we'll
never know*

MEOW OR MIAOW

Your bog-standard cat vocalization. Seldom used by adult cats in the wild but effectively adapted to get results from us humans. Cats work hard on developing a whole range of meows with different uses to communicate efficiently with their dense owners. *See also* COMMUNICATION, LANGUAGE

MEOW MONDAY

Guaranteed to brighten any Monday after a weekend curled up with your puss, there are no rules, just make it cute to banish those blues. #meowmonday *See also* CAT BOX SUNDAY, CATURDAY, FLUFFY FURSDAY, JELLY BELLY FRIDAY, KITTY LOAF MONDAY, TONGUE OUT TUESDAY, WHISKERS WEDNESDAY

MESSY EATERS

Our purr-fect pusses can be surprisingly messy eaters for such otherwise neat and meticulous animals. You may find half nibbled kibble strewn around or mushy lumps of wet food under your feet. It is in a cat's instincts to bite their prey and drag it off somewhere safe from pilfering, and this can lead to some 'interesting' food habits in the modern household. Try feeding your kitty in a quiet place away from other pets, with a nice shallow bowl and perhaps a mat, to improve their eating etiquette.

A happy, but messy, eater

Consider some relaxing mewsic

MEW

An endearing, high-pitched meow first observed as kittens but utilized throughout a cat's life, particularly when pestering is required. Pulls on the heart strings and likely to get results. *See also* DOORS, FEEDING TIME

MEWSIC

While our fuzzy companions may not appreciate our own musical taste, there are now many playlists and compositions available just for cats, and it seems music developed specifically for kitties, which mimics the frequency and speeds familiar to them from feline communications, is more likely to get a paws-itive reaction. *See also* LOUD NOISES, MATING CALL

MICE

Mice are a favourite target for our miniature killers – they are the perfect-sized toy, they are fun to stalk and can conveniently be gobbled whole. Grisly mouse gifts are generally the least frowned upon by their human friends. If your puss is too lazy to hunt, just having a cat in your home is enough to put most mice off moving in. However, don't relax too much – some cats have been known to bring live mice inside, who then quickly make themselves at home. *See also* GIFTS, HUNTING, PREY

MILK

Contrary to popular wisdom, milk is a-paw-rently to be avoided and can lead to upset tums. You can get special cat milk but be warned – it's very fatty and could quickly lead to a new chonk in the house, so save it for a treat. Kittens don't need their mother's milk after a very swift nine weeks but they'll never forget that kneading instinct and the comfort of their real cat mum. *See also* CHONK, KNEADING

MIRRORS

Research suggests cats don't understand they are seeing their own reflection in a mirror and a kitty confronted by one for the first time is certainly likely to experience an undeniably cute bushy tail moment. However, you can't fool our clever pusses for long and most cats soon learn there is something not quite right about these cats in the wall and will smartly treat them with nothing more than indifference or their usual disdain.

Mirrors: likely to cause a bushy-tailed moment

A public cat shaming may follow this misdeed

MISCHIEF

Climbing the curtains, deliberately knocking off objects, emptying drawers, unrolling loo paper, attacking the dog – all purr-fectly normal cat mischief and ingenious ways to get *your* attention. It is almost impossible but ignoring naughtiness and upping your cat's entertainment might help. *See also* CURIOSITY, DISCIPLINE

MISDEEDS

Like a modern-day shaming in the stocks, you can now air your dirty washing in public and disgrace your kitty on social media by declaring their misdeeds – alongside a photo of your puss looking suitably guilty – for all to see. From shredding tissues and destroying knitting to trampling over newly baked pies and digging up flowers, our criminal masterminds have a lot to answer for. #catshaming *See also* DISCIPLINE

MITTENS

A mitted kitty has little, usually white, paws. Mittens is accordingly a popular name for these sock-wearing felines. *See also* PAWS

MOGGY OR MOGGIE

A domestic cat of no particular breed or origin and by no means ordinary. Healthy and magnificent, our unique moggies come in every shape and size and will charm the kitty socks off you.

MOODS

A cat has all the emotions at their disposal and will appear to take great pleasure in swinging wildly and unpredictably from one to another to confuse and baffle us humans. A blissfully contented cat will surprise us with a sudden scowl or a swipe, and if only they could point their furry paws at a feelings wheel we might escape before the claws come out. Learn to read their signals and you will all be happier.

MOON PHASES

There is no scientific data to link a full moon with changes in our cats, but some owners report more feline high jinks on these nights. One study reported an increase in urgent vet visits on a full moon night, suggesting some additional mischief, so purr-haps there is some truth to it. *See also* MISCHIEF, ZOOMIES

MOPING

Our furry pals get down in the dumps sometimes just like us, and they might be feeling a bit under the weather, bored or even lonely. Or they could be simply punishing you for a recent cattery stay or another crime against cats. If you notice your cat is feeling blue and it doesn't pass quickly, talk to your vet – it could be physical or something lacking in their lives. Cats also grieve the loss of their humans or fellow pets and it can take time for them to feel better. *See also* ANXIETY, CATTERY, ILLNESS

NAMES

Studies reveal that cats do generally know their name, but whether they choose to respond is a different matter. (Most owners add to the confusion by using a whole array of nicknames for their furry friend.) Your cat may arrive with a name in tow from a shelter, but it should be OK to change it over time if it doesn't feel right for your new house guest. Choose wisely, for while it can cause much hilarity to give your cat an a-mews-ing name, your poor puss will have to live with your choice for a feline lifetime.

NAPS

It's all about the catnap. It can literally be carried out anywhere, anytime. Although your cat will have their favourite spots in your home, they like to mix it up with some novel locations that might include plant pots, pudding bowls, fire grates and wastepaper bins. More traditional factors such as comfort, warmth and suitability appear strangely irrelevant in these cases. *See also* BEDS, BEDTIME, SLEEP

Naps: anywhere, anytime, anyhow

Not purr-ticularly guilty:
snaffling the neighbour's food

NEIGHBOURS

Unfortunately, your outdoor cat may get up to some mischief when they are out and about and it can cause problems with your neighbours. Some cheeky cats will merrily help themselves to another cat's food, take a nap on a neighbour's sofa, use another garden as their own private bathroom, or much worse. Remarkably, some people take exception to these activities, and you and your cat may find yourselves in a spot of bother. Take a cat's approach to conflict resolution – talk it through and avoid a boxing match, if at all possible. *See also* FIGHTING

NEUTERING

An im-paw-tant rite of passage for every kitten, neutering generally happens between four and six months and is also known as spaying for females or 'the snip' for males. You might be apprehensive, but your puss will be well looked after, and your newly neutered pet will be at less risk of some cancers and disease and should grow up to be less aggressive and less likely to roam. Overrun cat shelters and their home-seeking inmates will also thank you for it. The cone of shame is certainly a memorable event in any cat household but it will soon be a distant memory for you both. *See also* CONE OF SHAME, COURTSHIP, MATING CALL

Night-time mischief

NIGHT-TIME

Cats will make no real distinction between night and day, it's all pretty much the same to them, and some determined felines will demand attention at all hours. As for most pesky puss behaviour, ignoring is your best bet, but it can be hard to pay no heed to a housemate that mews pitifully at your door, scales the blind or paws at your face in the depths of the night. *See also* ATTENTION, CREPUSCULAR

NINE LIVES

According to myths from all over the world, cats are the lucky possessors of multiple lives, most famously nine. How happy we would be if it were true. *See also* IDIOCY, MAGIC

Ninja skills in action

NINJA

Our mini ninjas are masters in martial arts kicks, stealth, ambushing, air acrobatics and unconventional tactics. Underestimate your kitty at your peril.

NORWEGIAN FOREST CAT

Rather like the Maine Coon but not quite as huge. Beautiful thick coats, majestic ruffs and fluffy ears keep them cosy in the winters while their fabulous whiskers and big eyes will melt your cold heart. *See also* MAINE COON, RUFF

The fluffy-eared Norwegian Forest Cat

A nose-to-finger nose-boop

NOSE-BOOP

Touching noses is used between cats as a friendly greeting. If you extend a finger to your cat they will often press their wet nose to it. If they lift their noses up towards yours, you might be the lucky recipient of a nose-to-nose cat kiss. Some cats are very free and easy with their kisses, while others reserve them for rare occasions. *See also* LOVE, SLOW BLINK

NUZZLE

There is nothing sweeter than the soft nuzzling of a cat's head against you. This sign of affection marks you with their scent, allows them to explore yours and will leave you with an all-over warm fuzzy feeling. *See also* NOSE-BOOP, SLOW BLINK

*Obedience: cats retain
the right to ignore you*

OBEDIENCE

Not really a word that we would associate with our fuzzy friends.
We know most cats are fiercely independent and not inclined to
follow our ridiculous commands, but paws-itive reinforcement can
work wonders in even the most headstrong of cats. It might surprise
you to learn that one study revealed cats value interaction above
food, so as always, play and attention may be the key to a happy and
therefore well-behaved puss. *See also* DISCIPLINE

ODD-EYED

These unusual eyes are most often found in Turkish Vans, Turkish
Angoras, Persians and Sphynx and commonly will be seen peeping
proudly from a white fur coat. Odd-eyed felines will have one blue
eye paired with a golden or emerald eye, and Turkish Angoras with
blue and amber eyes are purr-ticularly celebrated in Turkey.

The sleek and large-eared Oriental

ORIENTAL
Rather like a green-eyed Siamese but without the points, these
intelligent cats have large ears and will have plenty to tell you about
their day. *See also* SIAMESE

OUTDOORS
It is a good idea to gradually introduce your kitty to the wonders
outside, as it will blow their tiny minds to experience the
natural world for the first time, and young cats may need some
supervision to keep them out of mischief. If you choose to let
your adventurous kitty outside, make sure your cat is neutered,
vaccinated and microchipped before letting them loose. Keeping
them inside at night is often a happy compromise to reduce

hunting opportunities and keep them safer on the roads. The size of a feline's territory varies greatly between cats and environments. In built-up areas, there are more cats around, so territories are often quite small. Cats will also roam outside their territory and some cats will travel great distances in their quest for adventure. *See also* CAT FLAP, HUNTING, INDOORS

OXYTOCIN

Stroking our felines releases the famous bonding hormone in our bodies that is also released when we are in love, and a study revealed that higher oxytocin levels were also recorded in cats the more their owners positively interacted with them, so being with our beloved pets can be a paws-itive experience for us both.

Stroking our felines gives us an oxytocin hit

PADS

Those sweet leathery paw pads come in a whole range of colours, including black, pink, orange and grey. They are strangely appealing to humans but they are sensitive, so most cats won't appreciate you meddling with them. These ingenious mini cushions help cats land safely and scientists are trying to mimic them to protect less well-equipped humans when coming down to earth. *See also* TOE BEANS

PAPER BAGS

Your cat will appreciate any opportunity to get inside, or purr-haps on top of, a paper bag. Heaps safer than their plastic counterparts, environmentally friendlier and generally free, paper bags are an easy win and guaranteed to keep your cat entertained for a few seconds. These take-away lairs have the added bonus of being easy to tear to pieces. *See also* BOXES, IF I FITS I SITS, GROCERIES

PATROL

Cats will busily patrol their territory to defend it from intruders and may do this several times a day. Your puss will want to check significant sites frequently for new smells and potential threats. They may paw-trol the home too, checking everything is just as it should be. This might be why closed doors and cat flaps can seem like a cat-astrophe to your furry sentry. *See also* DOORS, HEDGEWATCH, OUTDOORS

Setting off on paw-trol

Paws in for a paw circle

PAW CIRCLE
If you or your feline are having a bad day,
send out an urgent request for a paw circle.
Be soothed as cats from around the world
obligingly send you pictures of their velvet paws
in the name of feline solidarity. #pawcircle

PAWS
Cats spend most of their time walking on their tip toes, which is
essential for sneaking around and speedy launches. Just like humans,
your cat may have a favoured front paw, maybe not for writing just
yet but probably for im-paw-tant investigations. *See also* CLAWS,
KNEADING, PADS, PAW CIRCLE, TOE BEANS

PEDIGREE
While there are many beautiful moggies needing homes, if you
have your heart set on a posh pedigree cat, make sure you do your
research on their character and needs and scrutinize the breeder's
practice. Some shelters report a rise in pedigree cats coming through
their doors, as breeds such as Bengals and Persians can be more
demanding than people realize. Due to the nature of their selective
breeding, pedigrees can also be more prone to disease, some more
so than others, so you need to take that into account. Take breed
personalities with a pinch of salt as all cats are individuals and we
know that cats don't like to conform if at all paws-ible. A dodgy
breeder will not raise a well-socialized and healthy kitten, so finding
the right breeder is well worth the wait. You could also consider
adopting a pedigree. *See also* ADOPTION, MOGGY

Persians: world famous floof

PERSIAN

World famous balls of floof, the Persian comes in many colour variations but they all have extravagant longhaired coats, short legs, snub noses and small ears. Mostly said to be sweet and mild-mannered, though their patience may be tried by the extensive grooming these fluffy cats require. The Exotic Shorthair is a Persian with all the features you would expect, such as the little ears and snub noses, but much less of the grooming.

PHEROMONES

When our cats rub their furry faces on objects and us, they are leaving behind an invisible form of chemical communication. Feline facial pheromones indicate a safe, secure place and there are artificial cat sprays and diffusers available that mimic them, which can prove useful for transmitting calm and serene vibes to your ruffled cat. Purr-ticularly useful for car journeys, vet visits and squabbling housemates.

Devious pill evasion

PILLS

Vets, of course, will make you feel like an incompetent fool and get a pill down your puss in seconds, with barely any complaint. Try this at home and all hell will undoubtedly break loose with your wilful friend. After a lengthy battle of nerves, generally involving a team-mate, towels, teeth and tears, you will sigh with relief when the pill has finally been safely swallowed. Meanwhile your sneaky feline will quietly eject the soggy pill and smugly saunter off until the next joust. If your furry friend is just too cunning, there are clever inventions such as pill poppers available to help you win the battle. *See also* DEVIL, DISPLEASURE, INTELLIGENCE

PLANTS

Greenery brings out the tiger in all our felines, so whether you have an indoor or outdoor cat, access to safe plants is a must for our little adventurers. Providing your cat with some fur-avourites, such as grass or catnip might deter them from attacking your precious houseplants. Watch out for enthusiastic cats scaling unsteady potted plants, and some plants are particularly toxic to our pusses so be careful. Pretty as they are, lilies should *never* be in the same home as a cat as they can do serious damage to your kitty's kidneys. *See also* CATNIP, GRASS, WILD

Eat, play, sleep, repeat

PLAY

For kittens, life is just one long loop of sleep-play-sleep-play but many people don't realize that adult cats need to play too. The problem is cats get bored with the same old games and you need to stay on your toes to keep them interested. Luckily a toy can be anything they can happily destroy, so even a ball of paper can prove a feline hit. Sometimes it can take the patience of a saint to engage your reluctant puss, and you may need to endure a very protracted stake-out before you get the long-awaited pounce. It's all about the hunt so any game that enables your puss to stalk, chase, pounce and mangle should bring hours of fun. 'Playing with the cat' is sadly often the last thing on your to-do list, but put in the effort and you will reap the rewards. *See also* TOYS

POINTS

A cat with points has a pale body with a dramatically contrasting face, tail and legs, and this unique feature has made the Siamese famous around the world. Rather fascinatingly, points are affected by the temperature, and although they are born white, as it is lovely and warm in the womb, pointed cats will gradually develop the darker patches in colder areas of their body from birth. Pointed coats come in a variety of colours, including the darkest seal point, chocolate, blue, lilac and red, and can be found in various breeds as well as the Siamese. *See also* RAGDOLL, SIAMESE

Stretching for purr-fect posture

POSTURE

Cats, of course, have purr-fect poise and they work hard to achieve their supple physiques. Our graceful friends look after their bodies with regular stretching throughout the day, plenty of those essential naps and hopefully some exercise. We could all learn from how dedicated cats are to the cult of the stretch. Whether they are sprawled out with belly joyfully exposed or hunched over in a bit of a grump, you can also read a great deal from our feline's posture of the day. *See also* COMMUNICATION, YOGA

POUNCING

Everyone's favourite bit of a pounce is obviously the bottom wiggle, observed just before the launch. Maybe it focuses all their senses, purr-haps it warms up those muscles after a long stalking session, or maybe it's an expression of excitement – the benefits seem unclear but there's no doubt it's cute. *See also* HUNTING, PLAY

PREY

Slightly horrifyingly, felines out in the wild would need to make between ten and twenty kills a day to survive, so our house cats are always poised and ready for a pounce. Favourite prey is generally smaller mammals and birds but some hunters will catch rats and even rabbits. *See also* BIRDS, HUNTING, MICE

PURRS

A sweet elixir for all cat lovers, the gentle purr comforts and relaxes us. This lovely sound comes from the voice box and is most often heard emanating from a contented puss, but it is also evident in other situations, and may be picked up when a cat is hungry or stressed, perhaps to self soothe. Kittens will melodiously purr away as they feed from their mother, and grown-up cats are often found purring while they knead. *See also* COMMUNICATION, KNEADING

PUSSYCAT

Yet another affectionate term for our fuzzballs but since it also describes a gentle person, it might be saved for their calmer moments. *See also* FUR BABY, MOGGY

Contented purrs while making dough

QUARRELS

Sometimes even the best of fur-iends can squabble. It's been observed by many multiple cat owners that a stay at the vets can cause the other cat or cats to throw a hissy-fit and reject them. If you have this problem, it might help to allow your returning puss some time alone to lick away those strange vet smells and replace them with their own purr-ticular scents so they are more recognizable to their housemates. Most quarrels are generally over access to the things dearest to them – food, attention and a safe place to rest their furry heads – so make sure they have their own resources and try not to intervene unnecessarily.
See also FIGHTING, FRIENDS, PHEROMONES

QUEEN

An unneutered female cat ready to bear kittens. Make sure she is always treated like the royalty she is. Left to their own devices, cats are seemingly inexhaustible breeders, and during breeding season she'll be in heat every two to three weeks.
See also COURTSHIP, DAM

QUILTS

Even though it must be stiflingly hot under there, cats will always try and sneak under a quilt or duvet for the ultimate snuggle and all the better if you're under there with them. Don't worry, they are purr-fectly capable of self-regulating and will make a swift exit if they get too hot under the collar. Dare to share your bed with them and they will soon be hogging all the covers, while you shiver under a measly corner.

The fluffy and floppy Ragdoll

RAGDOLL

These big cats conceal their powerful build behind a great deal of floof. They have satisfyingly big paws, lustrous tails and the pretty blue eyes of pointed cats. Ragdolls are renowned for their docile temperament. *See also* POINTS

RAIN

You might have a cat that hates the rain so much it will hide under the bed at the slightest drop; or your feline may love the excitement of a rain shower and charge outside to make the most of it. Although most cats will avoid rain, there are some that paws-itively enjoy a splash outside. *See also* WATER

RAINBOW BRIDGE

A mythical place where cats go when they die, awaiting their owners. #rainbowbridge

RANGE

Your cat may never leave your home or you may have a real adventurer on your hands, and the distances cats travel varies enormously. Tomcats will travel further to find potential lady friends but most neutered cats have smaller ranges. While some thrill seekers will go much further in the name of exploration, most house cats stay within 100 metres (109 yards) of home.

RANK

Some cats are naturally confident and self-assured and may have the swagger of a boss cat while others seem submissive and nervous. However, cats don't appear to have clear hierarchical social structures. Instead, different rules might apply for different resources in homes with multiple kitties. You might find one cat has the prime sleeping position on the radiator, while another might get first go at dinner time. If one dares to rip up the carefully agreed treaty, there might be some trouble. *See also* FIGHTING

RELAXING

Our friends are purr-ticularly good at relaxing if the conditions are just right, and that might mean a large dose of sunshine and no loud noises, depending on the purr-sonality of your cat. Classic signs of a relaxed feline include lying on their side with tummy exposed to the world, eyes softly closed, perhaps a tail gently flopping about. Of course, stroking our miraculous pusses is also relaxing for us. *See also* ANXIETY, LOUD NOISES, NAPS

Relaxed and feline good

RELIGION

Ever since cats weaved their furry way into our homes, they have also enjoyed the spotlight in religions around the world. For example, Bastet, an ancient Egyptian goddess of fertility, was depicted with a cat's head and often had feline attendants, while Hindu goddess Shashti sometimes appears riding a cat or even with a cat face. And Norse goddess Freyja rode a chariot drawn by cats. Some might say our modern worshipping of our felines has reached religious levels. *See also* ICONS, GODS & GODDESSES

RESCUE

You may find a cat at your door from time to time and sometimes it can be hard to know if they need help or are just a friendly cat hoping for some extra snacks. Keep an eye on them but if the cat looks healthy and a good weight, avoid feeding them. They might be microchipped so you can ask a vet to scan them, or you could post on social media and ask your neighbours if anyone knows them. A genuinely lost cat is likely to be disorientated and will try and get into homes to find food and shelter. *See also* ADOPTION, LOST

ROUTINE

From their elaborate grooming practices to their regular paw-trols, our fur-iends thrive on a constant and familiar routine. It makes them feel secure to know what their day holds. Observe your kitty and you will likely see they have developed their own little routine for the day to fit in nicely (or not so nicely) with yours. A study revealed that changes to a feline's routine or environment impact directly on their health, so it may help to introduce changes gradually. *See also* ANXIETY, BEDTIME, PATROL

Fur-iendly rubs

RUBS

Rather adorably, friendly cats will approach each other and rub their heads and bodies together – some may walk in step as they rub or perform the cute routine as they pass each other in opposite directions. Our felines will honour us too and greet their human, with tails up, with an affectionate rub. Sometimes a nearby chair will do the job instead. *See also* COMMUNICATION, LEG RUBBING, PHEROMONES

RUFF

Not the fad for, a-mews-ing to some, Elizabethan-style collars, but the natural ruff of fluff around the neck, often seen on semi-longhaired cats. Cats who can pull off a ruff with style include LaPerms and Ragamuffins.

RUNNING

Cats have a few running styles up their furry sleeves, including the amble for general pottering around, trotting for covering longer distances at a decent pace, and galloping for those turbo-charged chases or quick escapes from cat mischief. Galloping is often observed in the zoomies. *See also* ATHLETIC, ZOOMIES

RUSSIAN BLUE

These sophisticated grey beauties have lovely thick, short coats and mesmerizing green eyes. Often described as gentle, quiet and purr-haps on the sensitive side.

A velveteen Russian Blue

SAVING FACE

Cats are very proud and don't easily admit their mistakes, but don't worry about your puss, they will have learned even the most embarrassing events are easily covered up by a quick grooming session. See also IDIOCY

SCENT

Investigating scents and leaving them behind is almost a full-time job for our furry friends. As well as their super noses, our fascinating felines have an extra tool, called the vomeronasal organ in their nasal cavity, which opens into their mouths, for detecting chemicals. When investigating a scent, you may sometimes see your cat with its mouth open and even seem to lick the air. This may lead to an embarrassing blep situation. See also BLEP, PHEROMONES, SMELL, UNPLEASANT SMELLS

SCRATCH POST

If you don't provide a good enough scratch post, your beloved feline will soon make light work of your sofas, couches, curtains and furniture. Cats love a good scratch and they need to do it for their claws, stretching, territory marking and maybe simply for the joy of it. As always with our pesky playmates, they may opt to ignore your new purchase, but choose well and they may come to appreciate it. It needs to be tall enough for our fully stretched runner beans and sturdy enough to withstand a crazed clawing. See also CLAWS, COMMUNICATION, SOFAS

SHORTHAIRED

For all the floof around, it's easy to forget that most cats are shorthaired. Chunky or slonky, these wonderfully low-maintenance, independent felines are both pleasing to the eye and a pleasure to stroke. *See also* BALD, LONGHAIRED, SLONK

SHOW CATS

Coiffed, pampered and floofed, show cats, like all cats, know they are something special. But at the end of the day, cage adorned with rosettes or not, remember the cat show adage 'everyone takes the best cat home'. *See also* CAT SHOWS, PEDIGREE

SIAMESE

One of the most famous and recognizable breeds in the world, Siamese cats have distinctive slinky bodies and striking blue eyes. Originally from balmy Thailand, these chatty cats will do anything for a spot in the sun. *See also* POINTS

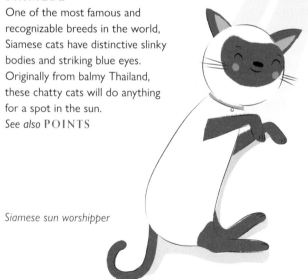

Siamese sun worshipper

Siberians: Kings and Queens of Floof

SIBERIAN

These big cats are the self-proclaimed champions of floof. Hailing from sub-Arctic forests, they have long, thick coats to protect them from the freezing winters of long ago. Contrary to their sneeze-inducing looks, they are said to be a good option for those with cat allergies. *See also* FLOOF

SLEEP

Many humans will be jealous of their cat's easy life, and it is not surprising when you find out our fluffy friends sleep an awe-inspiring twelve to eighteen hours a day. Although we are gravely advised never to interfere with a sleeping cat, they are experts at disturbing a sleeping human and will use any arsenal at their disposal, from enthusiastic purrs to face batting and curtain climbing. *See also* LAP CAT, NAPS

SLONK

A slinky, long-legged, slender cat, such as a Siamese or Oriental. Don't be complacent, however, for even slonky cats have been known to slide over to the chonky side. #slonk

SLOW BLINK

No honour is received more gratefully by a cat lover than the solemn but loving slow blink. Narrow your eyes and then gently close them and open them and your cat may slow blink in return. Use this method when approaching a new cat too and you are more likely to get a friendly response. Cat owners don't need evidence, but there is scientific research to confirm the slow blink is a paws-itive way for cats and humans to communicate. *See also* LOVE, NOSE-BOOP

SMELL

The feline sense of smell is fourteen times better than yours, and that was before Covid came along. Your cat will want to stick its nose into literally anything that enters the house to check it is up to cat standard. This is particularly im-paw-tant for shopping bags and boxes and it may be necessary to try them out for size too. *See also* GROCERIES, PHEROMONES, UNPLEASANT SMELLS

SOFAS

Also known as scratch posts, your couches, settees, loungers, sofas – or whatever you call them in your house – are a favourite attention-grabbing tool to display feline prowess. Bow down, watch and weep as they exercise those claws on your most expensive item of furniture. Throws and blankets are your friends.

SOLITARY

Our domestic cats are naturally solitary but have adapted to tolerate other cats and live alongside humans. It can be stressful for cats encountering other neighbouring cats every day and they generally try to avoid contact with each other. Most cats are content to be the only cat in the home, but many owners have more than one and some cats can be the best of fur-iends. Whether it's a peaceful experience for everyone depends on their individual purr-sonalities and environment. *See also* ANXIETY, FIGHTING, FRIENDS, PHEROMONES

SPHYNX

These highly intelligent cats can be traced back to an aptly named kitten called Prune. Owners with allergies may find these unusual cats more tolerable because there is less cat hair flying around, though they still produce the allergen that most people are allergic to. If they seem like the cat for you, be aware they need extra care, and love attention. *See also* BALD

SPOTTED
One of the main tabby patterns, with small or large spots that follow the classic vertical tabby stripes. *See also* MACKEREL, TABBY

SPRAYING
It's a very frustrating experience for everyone but try not to get cross with your errant cat. Spraying is different from going to the loo and is a normal feline behaviour outside, but if your cat is spraying inside, it could be a sign of stress. It often starts when a new animal joins the household or there's another change in their environment and you should check with your vet that there is nothing wrong. If your cat is squatting down, they need to empty their bladder, and you need to consider why they are not using their litter tray or going outside. Male cats, in particular, can develop a blockage preventing them from weeing, so if you see unproductive straining, take an urgent trip to the vet. Unfortunately for us, favourite alternative spots for going to the loo include sofas and duvets, and once they have used a spot it can be hard to stop the pesky pusses going back, so a thorough cleaning is essential. *See also* OUTDOORS, UNPLEASANT SMELLS

STARING
You may sometimes find your cat staring intently at you, often while you are absorbed in work or a pastime, and this can be disconcerting. Your cat is probably after something, whether it be play, dinner or just some fuss from you, and has learned that staring gets results. They could also be showing you affection and you may be lucky enough to get a slow blink if you look their way. *See also* SLOW BLINK

STRESS

Our fur-iends are rather stoic and can often hide signs of stress, but learn to read their body language and you can help keep them stress free. Be mindful of the things that all cats need – such as quiet places to eat and to go to the loo, a safe haven from loud noises, grabbing hands, overpowering scents and rival cats – to reduce the stress triggers in their lives. *See also* ANXIETY, SPRAYING

STRETCHING

A cat has a lot of sleeping to do, and after every nap comes the stretch routine. Our yoga buddies will spend a vast amount of their day contorting their bodies into an impressive array of positions. They will revel in the experience, and enjoy stretching every part of their bodies, from their ears to their toes. Classic positions include the front paw stretch with bottom up to the skies, the purr-fectly neat arch and the horizontal 'look how extremely long I am'.
See also ARCHING, YOGA

The 'look how extremely long I am' stretch

STRING

Something about that wiggling movement really gets a cat's hunting instincts revving. If your puss goes crazy for string, make sure you supervise any play with it, as they can ingest it or get dangerously caught up in it. *See also* TOYS, X-RAY

STROKES

All cats have their own purr-ticular likes, but favourite places to receive strokes are the cheeks, bottom of the ears and chin. It's quite common for cats to dislike some areas, such as their tummies, being stroked so look out for those positive kitty signals such as purring, rubbing and a relaxed demeanour. Some cats seem to delight in long petting sessions while others prefer a quick tickle. Every cat is unique, and bear in mind they might tolerate your strokes but not really enjoy them, so learn to read their body language. *See also* CUDDLES

SUNSHINE

Our solar-powered felines love to bask in the sun and they will make the most of any sunny patch, whether it's sprawled precariously on the window sill or spread-eagled on the lawn. However, just like us, cats can get too much sun, and you should keep an eye on pale-coloured cats in purr-ticular, who are more at risk of burning. Cats with white ears can suffer from a type of skin cancer caused by too much sun on their delicate ears. Make sure you have some shady spots outside and you can even get kitty sunscreen for those that are susceptible. *See also* HAPPINESS, HEAT

TABBY

Surprisingly, all our house kitties have the tabby gene but the distinctive stripes may not be visible in your purr-ticular moggy. The most common tabby pattern is the classic (blotched) with the attractive appearance of marbling, but there are also mackerel (striped) and spotted patterns. There are a range of colours, including red, brown and silver, and tabbies have an un-fur-gettable M shape on their foreheads. *See also* MACKEREL, SPOTTED

TAIL

What amazing accessories our felines possess. Whether floofy or sleek, the unassuming tail can pose as a handy toy, a mood barometer, a silent walkie-talkie, a balance pole or a threatening device. It can puff up to enormous size in an instant, it can signal everything from contentment through mild irritation to anger, and it is an endless source of wonder. *See also* ATTACK, COMMUNICATION, FLOOF, RUBS

Tails: fail-safe mood barometers

TALKING

The high-pitched baby voice many of us adopt when speaking to our cats is a slightly embarrassing side effect of being a cat owner but has been shown to be effective in getting our cats' attention. While many owners take advantage of a free therapy session and bore their cats with every detail about their day, some chatty cats wish to do the same and will have plenty to tell you after you've been apart. Neither will have a clue what the other is saying but it certainly seems to please both parties. See also CAT LADY, COMMUNICATION

TASTE

Taste is one of the rare occasions when humans are rather better equipped than our furry friends. Perhaps luckily for us all, cats do not possess a sweet tooth, and are unable to taste sweetness. There would likely be a few more chonks around if they could. Kittens are generally open to new tastes and will often wolf down any interesting flavours you put before them – after a thorough sniff, of course – but our adult fusspots tend to be more purr-ticular about their tastes. See also FOOD

TEETH

Amazingly, kittens teethe twice in a very short time and you may find your kitten chewing on everything in sight, including you. Unfortunately, our fanged beauties are rather prone to tooth decay and gum disease, but brushing their teeth will help. As with everything, starting when they are kittens is your best chance of completing this perilous challenge unscathed.

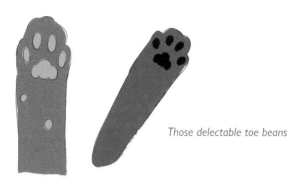

Those delectable toe beans

TOE BEANS
A fitting nickname for those little jellybean-like paw pads.
#toebeans *See also* PADS, PAWS

TOMCAT
Generally used to refer to those unneutered male rogues,
always getting in scraps and out looking for the ladies.
See also COURTSHIP, FIGHTING

TONGUE OUT TUESDAY
It's just not in keeping with their usual sophisticated selves to
witness a cat with their tongue hanging out. Nevertheless, many
felines are captured on film in this vulnerable moment and shared
for all to see. Luckily your cat will have no knowledge of this mild
humiliation. #tongueouttuesday *See also* BLEP, SCENT

TORTOISESHELL

Nicknamed Torties, these mostly female cats have a black coat with prominent ginger and red patches. Breeds with Tortie variations include Persians and Maine Coons. Purr-haps unfairly, they are sometimes credited with a fiery temper, and affectionately labelled the 'Norty-Torty'. *See also* CALICO

TOYS

From paper bags to curtains, everything in your home is a potential toy and your innovative cats are likely to put them all to the test in the pursuit of fun. Cats don't like to conform and will likely give your flash new kitty toys a wide berth. Sometimes the simplest homemade toys are the best, and if your cat is in the mood, a ball of paper will suffice. Fur-avourites in the shops include fishing rods and wagglers, tunnels and catnip-filled fabric mice and fish. They will also require your undivided attention while they play too, no peeking at phones allowed! *See also* ATTACK, LASERS, PLAY, STRING

TRAVEL

Unfortunately, there will come a time when you will have to travel with your cat. We've all seen adventure cats on social media, taking journeys in their stride, but most felines will find any trip a challenge, and will be sure to tell you this. Some cats will wail and moan the whole time while others will quietly suffer their fate. The wailers can try your patience, but keep calm, use your best reassuring voice, consider some mew-sic for cats and grit your teeth.
See also CARRIERS, CATERWAUL, MEWSIC

TREATS

Like their human friends, cats go crazy for the least nutritious snacks available. There are some best-selling treats that seem to hit the spot with most felines and they can be useful arsenal for getting your cat to comply. Make sure you stow these carefully away – some pussycats are ninja-like in their pursuit of these wondrous delicacies. *See also* TASTE, TRICKS, TUNA

TREES

It's a bit of a design flaw that our nifty felines are accomplished climbers when going up but are not quite so adept at getting down again. Our trouble-finding pusses can certainly get themselves into a spot of bother, often succumbing to the temptation of chasing squirrels or the like. Cats generally prefer to jump down but sometimes they go too high and only realize when it's too late. In most cases, they will eventually work it out, but it can be a nerve-racking experience for all. Try calmly calling from the bottom of the tree with some of their favourite food, and the temptation may be enough to entice them down. Sometimes they are well and truly stuck but, rather unbearably, owners are advised to wait an agonizing twenty-four hours before seeking help from an animal rescue service – sure to be the longest day of your life! Unsurprisingly, fire departments are keen to dispel the myth that they are available to rescue your wayward kitty. *See also* ALL-NIGHTERS, CLIMBING, LOST

With treats, anything is paw-sible

TRICKS

You *can* train your cat to perform a variety of tricks, from high fives to little jumps and cat kisses, and the internet is full of cute videos of cats doing exactly that, but would you want to? With clicker training and a hungry cat, anything is paw-sible and it will certainly cause much amusement, but the contrary nature of our felines is what makes them special to us and a spontaneous nose-boop or belly flop are all the tricks we need. *See also* AGILITY, TREATS

TRILL
The sweetest little noise from your furry friend, guaranteed to gladden the heart, this singy-songy sound is a bit like a high-pitched rolling rrrrrrrr. *See also* MEOW, PURRS

TUNA
So celebrated and loved by cats, it even has its own designated day, a rival for cute blep photos and a good fallback option when you can't capture your cat with its tongue hanging out. Keep tuna for a well-deserved treat. #tunatuesday, #tongueouttuesday
See also FISH, TONGUE OUT TUESDAY

TURKISH ANGORA
These handsome cats are highly celebrated in Turkey and are known for their foxy tails, silky coats and high intelligence. Despite the floof, they don't need too much grooming.

TURKISH VAN
Similar in looks to the Turkish Angora, but mostly white with a distinctive coloured tail and head markings. Apparently big fans of water.

UNPLEASANT SMELLS

Fortunately, our clean freaks don't often smell bad and would frankly be mortified to be the source of any unsavoury odours. However, nobody can deny that feline urine can smell pretty awful, and while most cats shouldn't feel the need to spray indoors, it might happen if you have a stressed puss and is more likely if you have more than one cat. Excluding any occasional passing of wind (even the most sophisticated of cats will succumb), if your poor kitty is the source of the stench, see your vet, as there are numerous health problems that can lead to a smelly cat. *See also* SPRAYING

URBAN

City cats must quickly learn to be street savvy if they're going outside, and as well as navigating busy roads they will have to bone up on social etiquette. They are likely to have to share territory with other neighbouring cats and will have to learn the delicate avoidance tactics our urban felines have developed. On the plus side, townie cats don't tend to roam as far, so they will be easier to track down at dinner time. *See also* COMMUNICATION, FIGHTING, OUTDOORS

VALERIAN

Less famous for its alluring properties than catnip, valerian can have similar effects on our cats. Purr-haps if catnip doesn't work its wonders on your kitty you could give a valerian toy a try! *See also* CATNIP

VAMPIRES

Our fanged, neck-biting merciless killers are, purr-haps unsurprisingly, frequently linked in popular folklore with vampires. It seems our fluffballs need merely to jump over a corpse or grave to turn any unfortunate mortal into a bloodsucking monster. In more recent times, it has been suggested by some that the Sphynx would make an excellent choice of pet for a vampire. *See also* BLACK CATS, SPHYNX, WITCHES

VANITY

Since it means having an excessively high opinion of oneself, we conclude cats are not vain. They evidently do have a high opinion of themselves but it's certainly not undue.

VELVET PAWS

Beneath our cats' beautiful soft inviting paws hide sharp claws. Don't ever forget it. *See also* CLAWS

VETS

A visit to the vet's is not on any cat's to-do list, in fact it is to be avoided by any means necessary. If you have an outdoor cat, you will forget to keep them inside and inevitably they will be nowhere to be seen while you anxiously watch the clock. If your cat is safely indoors, they will sneakily tuck themselves under a bed while you desperately try to entice them out. After a protracted battle at home getting them *into* the carrier, you can then enjoy an embarrassing scuffle to get them *out* of the carrier in front of your friendly vet. Fortunately, vets are pretty accomplished at this task and you may find they can do a much better job of it than you. Your cat will then creep around the room trying to find the most suitable hiding place, which might be crammed into a tiny sink, perched awkwardly behind a computer

Vets: a trip to be avoided at all costs

monitor or stuffed in a random drawer. Strangely, once captured, our fuzzballs often submit to the authority of the vet and allow them to perform the less than pleasing but miraculous things they need to do. *See also* CARRIERS, CONE OF SHAME, DISPLEASURE, PILLS, TRAVEL

VIEW
Cats love to watch the world outside from a nice warm vantage point, even if they can come and go as they please. Look-out duties are an im-paw-tant part of your sentry's day and there is much to inspect. While most felines will find a suitable window, consider a window hammock for those without sunny ledges to view from. Some pussycats will patiently await your return at the window, while keeping a watchful eye on the comings and goings outside. *See also* EYES, HEDGEWATCH

VILLAINS
Our fluffy friends are associated with witches, vampires, devils and now, in popular culture, with villains. With their sweet faces, fuzzy paws and beguiling purrs, it is hard not to let our little villains get away with anything they please. Purr-haps it is their mysterious aura or inscrutable demeanour that makes them such worthy accomplices in crime. *See also* DEVIL, GRIMALKIN, MISDEEDS, WITCHES

Washing is not welcome

WASHING

Who needs soap and water when you are purr-fectly evolved to do it all yourself? Cats spend countless hours cleaning themselves and can usually handle it all themselves just fine thank you very much, but occasionally they may need a little (unwelcome) assistance.
See also BATHS, LICKING

WASHING MACHINES

Whether it is the mesmerizing rotations, the comforting white noise or the warmth emanating from within, washing machines and tumble dryers have a certain allure that cats find hard to resist. Some cats love to get involved and will do anything for a roll in the warmed clothes fresh from the tumble dryer or a spot snoozing on the top. Keep the doors shut at all times, as some poor kitties have been known to accidentally endure a wash cycle after sneaking in for a cosy nap.
See also DISHWASHER, HEAT

WATER

Our felines can be very demanding when it comes to their water supply, and whatever you do will probably be the *wrong* thing, but you must try to please. Plastic bowls are a no-no – it doesn't taste so good – and their bowl must not be positioned near their food or their litter tray. As always, each cat in the household will appreciate their own water source. Some purr-ticular pussycats will prefer filtered water or even running water. Despite all your efforts, they will probably much prefer to drink from a puddle or a random plant pot.

Your water glass is always pre-furred

WATER GLASSES

Your water glass is *always* more appealing than their water receptacle. It just is. Even if you give them their own water glass, they will still pre-fur yours.

WEATHER

Old proverbs suggested a sneeze or a snore from a cat foretold bad weather, and many owners today swear their felines can predict a storm. Our super-sensitive cats are purr-haps more in tune with nature than us and always keen to avoid unnecessary exposure to the elements. As ever, our self-sufficient pets can adapt to most conditions, fluffing their fur in colder conditions and licking themselves cool in the stifling heat. Most cats will give Arctic weather a wide berth, but some cats, even slonky ones without much floof, will enjoy a play in the snow. *See also* HEAT

WET FOOD

Nobody can deny it has a foul aroma and a revolting texture, but many cats simply love their wet food, so you will have to push through the gross for your kitty's health and happiness. Watch out for the little lumps of food your pussycat will helpfully decorate the floor with. *See also* FEEDING TIME, FOOD, MESSY EATERS

WFH

The advent of working from home has been a challenge for all cats. Some are bewildered by the intrusion into their space, while others are delighted with their new daytime playmates. While some cats are content to snooze nearby while you work, others have quickly evolved to find new creative ways to grab our attention. From zoom-bombing your meetings, to warm chair-hogging and theatrical keyboard-flopping, our cats are adept at distraction and look set to continue making hard work of our new working arrangements. #wfh. *See also* ATTENTION

Zoom-bombing, an essential skill for the new WFH era

WHISKERS

One of the most appealing features of our beautiful felines are their long white whiskers, and although most famously positioned next to their noses, they are also above the eyes, on the chin, by the ears and at the back of their front legs. Whiskers are long, thick hairs with very deep roots and are mostly white. These ingenious devices have many purposes and help cats navigate in the dark, fit through tiny gaps, detect their prey close-up, and communicate their moods. Although you must not cut whiskers, they do sometimes fall out and will grow back, so don't fret if you find one.

WHISKERS WEDNESDAY

A mid-week chance for a flattering close-up of your beloved feline to show off their impressive whiskers. The longer, the better, but all are purr-fectly welcome. #whiskerswednesday
See also CATURDAY, CAT BOX SUNDAY, FLUFFY FURSDAY, JELLY BELLY FRIDAY, KITTY LOAF MONDAY, MEOW MONDAY, TONGUE OUT TUESDAY

WHITE CATS

Purr-ticularly popular with pedigree owners, these eye-catching pussycats are certainly memorable. They are famous both for their work assisting villains, and good luck, as seen in the depiction of Japanese maneki-neko figurines. Unfortunately, white cats can be prone to deafness, especially those with sparkly blue eyes. *See also* PERSIAN, TURKISH ANGORA, VILLAINS

White cats, bound to enjoy a roll in the dirt

WILD

Whether it's slinking about behind the curtains or trampling through your favourite flower beds, our pampered house cats will quickly imagine themselves back in the jungle. There is very little separating our domesticated darlings from wild-cats, and DNA analysis reveals that the most differences are in their purr-sonalities. Cats haven't really had to adapt to domestication, and some suggest instead that it was our cats that domesticated *us* all those thousands of years ago and have been living in the lap of luxury ever since. *See also* BENGAL

WISDOM

Cats are renowned and celebrated for their wisdom and they can certainly seem wise beyond their years. They approach life with an ease and openness we can all admire. They express their feelings easily, avoid conflict, find time for play and rest, and live in the moment. However, caution is advised in following their advice, for there is no denying they can be pretty daft too. *See also* INTELLIGENCE, X-RAY

WITCHES

Long associated with witches, cats, and especially black cats, have had a troubled history. It was believed in the Middle Ages that witches could transform into cats and widely thought that cats were their evil assistants – their familiars – a suspicion still alive today with the feline role of villain's side kick. Independent and impervious to authority, it is perhaps no surprise our furry friends have ruffled the feathers of those who seek to control and suppress. *See also* BLACK CATS, CAT LADY, DEVIL, GRIMALKIN, MAGIC, VILLAINS

X-RAY

It can be hard to believe our clever pussycats would be so stupid, but it seems felines are notorious for swallowing strange objects. Popular targets include wool, rubber bands and hair ties. An annual competition has revealed X-rays showing a bizarre series of ingested items, including an entire guitar string, an astronaut pendant and the feet of a rubber lizard toy. The advice is don't trust your cat *not* to eat it, because they just might.

XXL

Ignoring the chonky cats for a moment, if you like your cats on the extra large size, you might want to consider some of the heavyweight breeds such as the Maine Coon, Siberian, Norwegian Forest Cat and Ragdoll. That's a whole lot of cat to cuddle.

YAWN

Cats take great pleasure in their extravagant and copious yawns and they all have their little idiosyncrasies when doing so. Some, a little alarmingly, keep their eyes open, while others will stick their tongues out, but all cats are a-mew-sing while yawning. They also purr-ticularly enjoy yawning in your face. *See also* JAWS

YOGA

While cats are deadly serious about their own yoga sessions and would frown on any interruptions, dare to get on a mat while your feline is around and you'll soon be cursing their bendy bodies. Whether they climb on your back, bite your hair, purr in your ear, or zig-zag beneath you, they just *have* to get involved. They might even demonstrate how it's done if you're really lucky. *See also* ATTENTION, STRETCHING

YOUTH

It can come as a shock to many new cat owners when their sweet kitties swiftly become unruly and sullen teenagers. They will push all the boundaries, just like any self-respecting teenager would, from staying out late to grunting monosyllabically and purr-haps skulking off to their bedrooms. This difficult phase of a cat's life lasts a surprising amount of time, starting around six months old, and could continue until they reach their second or third birthday. Hopefully, at the end of this challenging chapter, a calm, affectionate and wiser pussycat will emerge. *See also* AGEING, KITTENS

YOWLING

Whether you call it yowling or howling, this is an impressively ear-splitting sound from our friends, often deployed when confronted by a territory rival. Both cats will go for it and the nerve-testing racket can be sustained for some time. Often these howling contests will be resolved without the need to progress to fisticuffs. *See also* CATERWAUL, FIGHTING

YUCK

Our furry friends are very sensitive souls and even a whiff of a yucky food, like a lemon or a tomato, or a strong odour such as an air freshener, can make cats gag in dramatic fashion. A-paw-rently, some cats react like this to certain sounds too. *See also* CITRUS, LOUD NOISES, YUM

YUM

Every cat has a key to their heart, and whether it is shop-bought treats or tinned tuna that drives them purr-ticularly wild, you can enrich their lives by offering new things to try. Much of it will inevitably be deemed yucky but you never know what might hit the spot. *See also* FOOD, TREATS, YUCK

ZIG-ZAG

This attention-grabbing manoeuvre is a skill most cats have mastered. A-paw-rently trying to trip you up as you walk around is an excellent way to get fed.

ZIPS

Some pointed cats get a cute darker zipper mark down their tummies, in true onesie style.

ZOOMIES

A spontaneous explosion of madness from your cat, often helpfully occurring when you are going to sleep. Their whole body will twitch with energy, they will race from room to room and dramatically overreact to the slightest thing. Curtains will be climbed, carpets clawed and sofas mounted. Don't try to reason with your manic moggy – they are possessed by a force stronger than you. *See also* CREPUSCULAR, INSANITY

ZZZ

How fitting this cat lovers' dictionary should end here – with a snooze. *See also* BEDS, BEDTIME, NAPS, SLEEP

Sweet dreams, kitty

ACKNOWLEDGEMENTS

This book is dedicated to my amazing partner, Ed, and inspiring daughters, Edie and Rosa, for their endless support. Without them, this project of my dreams would never have come to be, and I could not have done this without their constant cheerleading and insightful feedback. I can't thank them enough.

I am extremely grateful to my brilliant agent Euan Thorneycroft at A.M. Heath for his unerring professionalism, encouragement and for believing in me and the book. Thanks also to Jessica Lee for her support.

Emma Foster gave skilful feedback from a vet's point of view and her helpful suggestions were greatly appreciated, but any errors are entirely mine. Thank you to Tess Lamacraft, Kath Stathers and Suzanne McNabb for the introduction to Emma, and to everyone at The Neighbourhood Vet for their first-rate care of Cookie.

A huge thank you to my wonderful editor, Sarah Thickett, for commissioning the book and for her enthusiasm and vision. Sarah and all the team at Quadrille have been an absolute pleasure to work with and I could not have found a better home for the book. Particular thanks to Claire Rochford, Wendy Hobson, Sabeena Atchia, Sarah Epton, Jonathan Baker and to everyone in the sales, marketing and comms team for all their hard work on the book.

Thanks to all the Small Dots clients and customers for their support and to the following for their general paws-itivity about the book: Nicola, Pete, Helen, Rich, Holly, Jim, Nik, Jane, Jo, Gillian, Jess, Katie, Pauline, John, Cynthia, Martin, Marjorie, Madelon, Valerian, Amanda, Steven and Antonia.

For further reading, I would recommend the information-packed Cats Protection website (www.cats.org.uk) and these excellent books, which have all been valuable resources in researching *The Cat Lover's A to Z*: *Cat Sense* by John Bradshaw; *The Cat: A Natural and Cultural History* by Sarah Brown; *The Complete Encyclopedia of Cats, Cat Breeds & Cat Care* by Alan Edwards; *The Complete Cat* by Vicky Halls; and *The Secret Language of Cats* by Susanne Schötz.

Our heartfelt thanks to the following cats for their invaluable snoopervision during the making of this book.

· HENRY & LYRA ·

Fur-avourite food: Lyra's and mice
Snoopervised: Euan

· COOKIE ·

Mostly found:
on paw-trol
Snoopervised: Clare

· BASIL ·

Also known as:
Bazzy Boo
Snoopervised: Emma

· FINLEY ·

Pre-furred sleeping
spot: in the sunshine
Snoopervised: Alicia

· ATTICUS & MISS MAUDIE ·

Also known as: Catticus & Good Girl
Snoopervised: Sabeena

· JUNO ·

Mostly found:
biting toes
Snoopervised: Katie

DJ & TIGER LILY

Pre-furred sleeping spot: someone's lap
Snoopervised: Wendy

HERCULES

Also known as: His Lordship
Snoopervised: Claire

HAMLET

Fur-avourite food: butter
Snoopervised: Humayra

MEEKO & LAFAYETTE

Also known as: Mikachu & Toot Toot
Snoopervised: Rebecca

Mostly found: licking
the hob clean
Snoopervised: Emily

PEACH

CHARLIE

Also known as: The Mewler
Snoopervised: Stephen

MIMI

Also known as:
Mimmy Moo
Snoopervised: Alex

Clare Faulkner is a freelance graphic designer and the illustrator of the best-selling *The Little Book of Sloth Philosophy* and *The Little Book of Otter Philosophy*. Following a career in book publishing, which included 10 years at the V&A, Clare retrained in graphic design. She has worked for a diverse range of clients, on book, brand and product design with her company Small Dots. Clare lives in London with her family and a mischievous Siamese cat, who is the inspiration for this book.

MANAGING DIRECTOR Sarah Lavelle
COMMISSIONING EDITOR Sarah Thickett
COPY EDITOR Wendy Hobson
PROOFREADER Sarah Epton
HEAD OF DESIGN Claire Rochford
HEAD OF PRODUCTION Stephen Lang
PRODUCTION CONTROLLER Sabeena Atchia
TYPESETTING Seagull Design

First published in 2023 by Quadrille,
an imprint of Hardie Grant Publishing
Quadrille
52–54 Southwark Street
London SE1 1UN
quadrille.com

The content of this book is the opinion of the author and is not intended as a substitute for professional medical advice, diagnosis or treatment. Always seek the advice of a qualified vet with any questions you may have regarding a medical condition.

Cataloguing in Publication Data: a catalogue record for this book is available from the British Library.

ISBN 978 1 83783 107 4

Printed in China

MIX
Paper from
responsible sources
FSC™ C020056